THE
EXPERIENCE
OF
LEADERSHIP

THE
EXPERIENCE
OF
LEADERSHIP

Proven Examples from
Successful Leaders

FRED STUVEK JR.

For information about this title or to order other books and/or electronic media, contact the publisher:

Triumvirate Press
617 W Main Street
Knoxville, Tennessee 37902
TriumviratePress@gmail.com
www.fredstuvek.com

ISBNs:
978-1732306073 (softcover)
978-1732306080 (eBook)

Publisher's Cataloging-In-Publication Data
(Prepared by The Donohue Group, Inc.)

Names: Stuvek, Fred, Jr., author.
Title: The experience of leadership : proven examples
    from successful leaders / Fred Stuvek Jr.
Description: Knoxville, Tennessee : Triumvirate Press, [2021]
Identifiers: ISBN 9781732306073 (softcover) | ISBN 9781732306080 (ebook)
Subjects: LCSH: Leadership. | Success. | LCGFT: Essays.
Classification: LCC HD57.7 .S78 2021 (print) | LCC
    HD57.7 (ebook) | DDC 303.34--dc23

Printed in the United States of America

Cover and interior design: 1106 Design

Contents

ACKNOWLEDGMENTS

Bringing this project to fruition required two things: One, selection. Two, selling. By "selection," I mean identifying those individuals I believed would best fit into this book. By "selling," I mean convincing them about the viability and value of this project, as without the participation of such a quality cast, it would not have been possible. I recognize this and would like to thank everyone who helped to make this possible.

I sincerely appreciate: Albert M. Calland III coming out of the shadows, so to speak, and agreeing to give us his views on leadership. Bert's story is the stuff of legend, and, to the best of my knowledge, this is the first time that he has agreed to put this to print. Bert is a national hero in the War on Terror, and our nation is indebted to him for his service and his sacrifice.

Steven Mays, whose assistance in this project has been of incalculable value. Steve has been with me through this entire journey and has been an outstanding resource on many fronts. Steve unhesitatingly took on many functions, such as reading drafts, providing input on concepts and ideas, helping to design covers, unfailingly conveying his keen insight, and offering advice. He never hesitated to take that contrary position which is so necessary to the improvement and success of any project.

He was also emphatic about having "less sizzle, more steak." Thank you, Steve!

John Ballard, for being meticulous and demonstrating a knack for picking up on the things that go unnoticed by others. John was instrumental in helping to pick out the title and subtitle and, along the way, made some valuable observations and recommendations which undoubtedly improved the quality of the book.

John "Boomer" Stufflebeem, for coming onboard and always being there when a question was asked or a sounding board needed. I recall his email, which is classic Boomer—concise, to the point, and difficult to misunderstand—when approached about the project. He simply responded "I'm in. Hooyah, Boomer." Boomer was an outstanding resource in referring some of the individuals in this book; he provided guidance and counsel throughout this process.

Jacob Kashiwagi, for your keen insight, analysis, and boundless enthusiasm. You were a constant presence throughout and never hesitated to provide input and make suggestions, to the betterment of this project. You are a pioneer in youth development, and those young folks are better for having you mentor them.

Torie Clarke, for buying into this project and making it work, regardless of what city or continent you were on. I enjoyed reading and discussing your stories, insight and perspectives on leadership, and advice on communication, especially during a crisis. I admire your understated manner and humility, considering all that you have accomplished, and appreciate you always exhibiting a creative and can-do demeanor.

Mordecai Brownlee, for taking that leap of faith to join this project and pointing out that "five stars always beats one star." Your passion for taking care of the people certainly comes through in your chapter. I wish you continued success in your new position.

Michael Miller, for coming onboard, exhibiting patience and understanding, and offering your perspectives on leadership. You are a student of leadership and well versed in many ideas and theories concerning the topic. I appreciate you sharing those with me, as I gained additional insight and perspective by collaborating with you.

Thomasina Skipper, for sharing your heartfelt journey, which is remarkable and could be a book unto itself. Your story will be a source of inspiration and motivation to many. You provide some great advice that is worth taking to heart.

Chris Molina, for your staunch belief and support in all things concerning leadership and for understanding that, if you never ask, you never know. You are passionate about the topic of leadership and will also always be one other thing: Once a Marine, always a Marine. *Semper Fi!*

Daralee Barbera, for your contribution, insight on leadership, and sharing your views with us. The readers will benefit from your lessons learned, as you pioneered the way on numerous fronts. And, by the way—congratulations on recently attaining your Ed.D.

Jon Rennie, for your ardent support and excitement about this project and all things leadership. I have enjoyed how you have shown that leadership practices in a submarine work in real life, although it is a much different environment, where there are only two types of ships, according to Jon—submarines and targets.

Carl Sharperson, for coming onboard, sharing your story with us, and exhibiting class and humility in all aspects of your life as you always take care of those around you. I have a great title for your sequel: "Razor Sharp Leadership."

Jackie Freedman, for taking that leap of faith, exhibiting enthusiasm with this project, and sharing your story. You have a knack for that attention to detail, all the while maintaining the broader perspective. You must get to Delicious Orchards.

Alan Lerchbacker, for not only agreeing to be in the book but working with me to set up the leadership classes with the University of San Diego. With your high-octane approach to life and a mindset that understands that all things are possible, you were an absolute pleasure to work with.

The students of the leadership class at the University of San Diego. I enjoyed talking with you, answering questions, and reading your responses. I wish each one of you all the best as you embark on your journey, hopefully avoiding anyone who exhibits Dark Triad personality traits.

INTRODUCTION

WHAT DEFINES GOOD LEADERSHIP, and how can we become *great* leaders? That is the essence of any leadership journey. As you embark on your leadership quest and seek answers, I want to help you in discovering something, which may or may not be apparent, but which I hope will be by the time you are done reading this book. We don't become great leaders by accident. We *learn* to be great leaders—often by the example of others. If leadership interests you and you are committed to learning best practices and principles, continue reading.

When I sat down to create *The Experience of Leadership,* I knew I wanted to put something together that would be different from other leadership books—a book that goes beyond inspiration and insights to offer the reader clear guidance on how to best develop their own leadership skills. Just as important, I wanted to show readers how they can continue to improve their skills, as we are always learning and growing. The "what" was there, but the "how" was something I wrestled with, as I wanted to accomplish three things with this book:

1. Help the reader become a great leader by learning new perspectives on leadership.
2. Provide guidance on principles and practices that have been proven to work in a number of environments.
3. Motivate and inspire the reader.

I wanted to cut through the generalities and nostrums about leadership and dive into the nitty-gritty details of how to obtain the experience and skills that great leaders display and aspiring leaders can learn from. So, I assembled a broad, diverse group of individuals who have attained success in various arenas in order to understand how their leadership journey unfolded—piece by piece. While most leadership books focus on leaders in the business world, highlighting titans of industry and celebrities, the crucible of leadership resides in areas that everyone has a great deal of experience with, has touched all of our lives, and is where most of life's leadership lessons are learned. It is in the crucible where the ore is refined so that it can be shaped into a useful tool, just as it is with leadership. Areas such as the military, education, and the sports arena come to mind, first and foremost, since it is here that the basic principles are imbued. These principles apply in any venue, across any platform. If your basics are sound, you are sound. Everything you do or learn from a leadership perspective has its origins in these camps.

It is not a coincidence that I mention the military and put it first on the list. There is tremendous value and benefit to having military experience. It has had a lasting impact on me, and I am thankful for the experience. I learned a number of lessons and values that had a direct and positive impact on my leadership endeavors throughout my life. It is the best arena for learning and developing leadership skills. Why is that? In the military, three things combine to forge a leadership journey. The first is the intensity of the demands. The necessity to make life-and-death decisions as well as decisions that affect millions or billions of dollars provides the intensity (the fire of the crucible). The second is the need to develop teamwork. You place your life in another's hands and ask them to place theirs in yours (the ingredients in the crucible). The third is the ability to adapt and change as circumstances change (adapting to the different elements in the ore to achieve the needed refinement). There is no better place than the military to encounter all of these conditions so early in a career.

Education shapes all of our futures. Every teacher is a leader. They lead by example and set the standard by the way they conduct themselves, how they communicate, and how they handle the needs of each and every student. In addition to the work in the classroom, they also have a profound impact in the community, influencing and enriching our lives. They also are mentors, providing counsel and insight that help their students chart their course and find their own way.

Playing sports is another area where leadership skills are developed. You learn the value of teamwork and how everyone's role contributes to collective success. You understand the value of practice and preparation. You develop the self-discipline required to acquire the skills. You experience adversity and learn to how to cope with failure. You learn to understand that, while a loss is a setback, you learn from it and become better prepared.

John F. Kennedy stated, "Leadership and learning are indispensable to one another." That is certainly my hope here. By learning from the achievements of those men and women featured in *The Experience of Leadership*, you will be acquiring insight and knowledge that will be indispensable to you on your leadership journey.

CHAPTER ONE

ALBERT M. CALLAND III

★ ★ ★ ★ ★

My View of Leadership from
Thirty-three Years as a Navy SEAL

Vice Admiral (VADM, retired) Albert M. Calland III ("Bert" or "Melrose" to friends) was born in Columbus, Ohio, and raised in Zanesville, Ohio, where he was a star three-sport letter winner in high school. He was an oceanography major at the US Naval Academy (USNA) and was a three-year starter on the Navy football team. He still holds the USNA record for most receptions in a season, is second in all-time career receptions, and was the team MVP his senior year. Following graduation, he was selected and qualified as a Navy SEAL. During his thirty-three years of active duty, VADM Calland served in numerous unique positions of national significance and impact. In 1987, he deployed to the Arabian Gulf in support of Operation Earnest Will as Commander, Naval Special Warfare Task Unit, Pacific, aboard a mobile sea barge, conducting interdiction and capture missions

*utilizing a variety of joint airborne and seaborne assets.
He commanded Navy Special Warfare Development
Group, a Chief of Naval Operations (CNO) Priority
One Major Command as well as Navy Special Warfare
Command, in charge of all Navy SEALs. VADM Calland
was Special Operations Commander Central Command
(SOCCENT) when the terrorist attacks of September 11,
2001, occurred. He directed, in-country, more than 3,000
US and Coalition Special Operation forces in support of
Operation Enduring Freedom. This effort included direct
and first in-country liaison and arrangements with the
current controlling factions in Northern Afghanistan for
entry and operation of Coalition Special Forces throughout
the campaign region. He was, literally, the initial "tip of
the spear" in the War on Terrorism, directing with boots-
on-the-ground the successful victory over the Taliban
regime. VADM Calland was appointed Deputy Director
of the Central Intelligence Agency by President George
H. Bush in July 2005 and served until he was specifically
selected, in July 2006, as Deputy Director for Strategic
Operational Planning at the National Counterterrorism
Center to set up and develop that organization. Following
retirement from the Navy, VADM Calland continued
his involvement in counterintelligence and the War on
Terrorism as Executive Vice President for security and
intelligence integration at CACI International Inc.*

★ ★ ★ ★ ★

THE TOPIC OF LEADERSHIP AND DIRECTING PEOPLE or
an organization to accomplish a goal, or whatever definition

you want to pull from the internet, old-fashioned dictionary, or the multitude of books, presentations, class notes etc., on the subject has been around for a long, long time, and I don't really believe I have anything unique to add to these already adequately expressed characteristics and advice. I have some personal experiences—or "sea stories," as we sailors call them—where I have utilized some leadership techniques that might be worth reviewing. However, we could shorten the whole discussion by just reviewing some historically proven guidance on leadership. If you want to know how some very successful "leaders" managed that success, you can simply read their printed advice. In fact, a detailed, interesting, and proven course of instruction on leadership could easily be put together based on historical quotes by proven leaders. One of history's most storied leaders, Winston Churchill, gives a wonderfully witty abundance of information on leadership. If you just successfully implemented the wisdom in his advice, you would be a more-than-adequate "leader": "You ask, what is our aim? I can answer in one word. It is victory, victory at all costs, victory in spite of all terror, victory, however long and hard the road may be; for without victory, there is no survival."

Few of us will ever face the absolutely dire situation and world catastrophe facing Churchill and his nation, but the intent is simply stated and leaves little doubt for interpretation. He knew that goals are easy to describe but also that the strategy to achieve them and attention to detail in executing that strategy are even more important. He also had another piece of advice that might fit numerous leadership situations: "Tact is the ability to tell someone to go to hell in such a way that they look forward to the trip." This emphasizes the point that, oftentimes, it is not only what you say but how you say it and, just as importantly, how you inspire those under your command.

Although I am not a big General Douglas MacArthur fan, as he was a little too flamboyant for my tastes, he had some excellent advice that certainly fit my perceptions of a good leader. "A true leader has the confidence to stand alone, the courage to make tough decisions, and the compassion to listen to the needs of others. He does not set out to be a leader but becomes one by the quality of his actions and the integrity of his intent."

General Colin Powell, another tried-and-tested leader, also had a number of great observations on leadership that could also form the basis of an outstanding course of instruction. I'll limit my reference to this very simple statement: "Great leaders are almost always great simplifiers, who can cut through argument, debate, and doubt, to offer a solution everybody can understand."

Finally, one of my favorite quotes from my "History of War, Colloquium" class at the U.S. Naval Academy (USNA) is by Alexander the Great: "I am not afraid of an army of lions led by sheep; I am afraid of an army of sheep led by a lion." And despite my contention that a good leader should build a team that can ably function without him or her, Alexander cleverly points out that leadership can be so very critical to success! (On a personal note, I was a huge Alexander fan and even named my first "new" sports car after the world conqueror.) To see the proof in Alexander's statement, you can look at how much of an impact the head coach of any sports team makes to the team's success or consider the number of generals President

Lincoln went through in our Civil War before U.S. Grant found success and victory.

I will just say right now, at the very beginning of this narrative, that my leadership style, my personality, and my journey through life is and has been all about three principles. First and foremost, **Integrity**—simply stated: do the right thing, be transparent up and down the chain of command, admit errors, try to repair them, and don't repeat them. Secondly, **Teamwork and Team Building**—create/be part of a team that is motivated to perform to the best of individuals' abilities to hopefully accomplish the assigned task, with or without active guidance, I might add. Thirdly, making what I call **"Quality Decisions"**—those junctures/situations in your life/career/assignment where you need to make something happen for the better. I will be focusing my discussion mainly in these three areas; I will give some personal experiences and try to explain how they line up with the commonly accepted attributes of good leadership. I also want to say upfront that I was extraordinarily fortunate to serve with an outstanding group of teammates in most of my leadership assignments; the successes I attained in a long career were due as much to their superior attitudes, support, and amazing performance as to my leadership competence! And, to emphasize a point I will make throughout this discourse, in the military, you get a lot of leadership training and assistance; so, I am going to list here, at the beginning, those leadership competencies that were part of one of the earliest leadership courses I took while in the Navy, including Leadership and Management Education and Training (LMET) courses. The myriad competencies listed for an effective leader were someone who: Sets

Goals and Standards, Takes Initiative, Plans and Organizes, Optimizes Use of Resources, Delegates, Monitors Results, Rewards, Disciplines, Exercises Self-control, Influences, Team Builds, Develops Subordinates, has Positive but Realistic Expectations, Understands, and Conceptualizes. While that is a fairly exhaustive list, throughout my career, I was able to incorporate most of these "competencies" within my smaller and easier-to-remember mantra of "**Integrity, Teamwork**, and **Quality Decision Standards.**"

I am a 1974 graduate of the U.S. Naval Academy, where I also I played football all four years. It was there where my military leadership training started, as the military schools are all about training young men and women to become leaders in military service after graduation. This culminates in your senior or first-class year. This is the year where you are truly in a leadership role, as this class leads the other three underclasses in all daily activity and competition; it was during this time I commanded one of the six battalions in the brigade. The lessons learned while at the Academy establish the baseline that you are able to build upon, as, after graduation, you are immediately placed in supervisory positions with leadership roles. While you certainly receive a great deal of leadership and management training, the required leadership skills and personality are not fully in place. This highlights the need to start out in a measured and disciplined manner while taking in all the lessons learned and continually adapting to the types of people you will lead, the complexity of the mission, the ever-changing landscape, emergence of threats—some seen, and some not so discernible—and the need to ensure alignment with a host of factors which also need to be considered! This is different from most other leadership positions such as sports teams, industry, exploration expeditions, leading protests/ riots, etc., where parameters are more fixed, variables are fewer, and outcomes not as critical. All of this reinforced to me that leadership is a continual learning experience that never really ends until you are no longer in a leadership position and just trying to figure out where your next fishing or golfing trip will take you. I was in leadership roles and leadership-learning situations for the next forty years of military and corporate assignments and was learning the entire time.

My leadership training started well before entering the Naval Academy, which leads to the question often asked as to whether leaders are born or developed. In my opinion, I contend the answer is a little bit of both. Some people are "born" with or develop early, more confident and outgoing personalities. They might seek out class-officer positions or, conversely, might become a class bully if popularity is an issue and they have not been given the right parental influence. Certain people have a stronger desire to assume leadership roles and take on political or social responsibilities. Confidence is definitely required to be a good leader in any of these roles, but it does not make you a good leader, does not give you good decision-making skills, does not teach you how to treat other people, and does not teach you integrity and honesty. Those traits begin at home, and that is where my leadership training began, with Nancy and Al Calland, my parents. They nurtured my competitive spirit, supported my athletic drive, taught me that winning isn't always the goal, to always strive to do your best, to treat people fairly and with respect, and, most importantly, they required **honesty and integrity** from

me in all aspects of my young life. They also instilled in me
the necessity for developing good habits. One of these habits
was being on time, which reminds me of a comment from
General Tommy Franks, someone I worked with and respect
a great deal: "If you can't take responsibility for your own life
and show up on time, you have no right leading anyone else.
Don't *ever* be late." Consequently, early on, I was always cognizant of the time issue and prided myself on being prompt. My
parents also held me accountable for my decisions. I learned
there are consequences to decisions and that it cuts both ways.
Decision-making is a part of everyone's life, and, here, I have
made a distinction. I call them **"quality decisions" instead
of "good decisions,"** because not all choices made with good
intent end up being a good call. Quality decisions are the best
choice you can make after careful analysis of all the available
information. That's the key, isn't it? Available information and
careful analysis of all the options/risks/outcomes.

I had an early experience with quality decisions when I was
ten years old. We had just moved to Columbus, Ohio, for my
Dad's job. This was my first introduction to public swimming
pools, and I did not know how to swim. After watching everyone splashing around and having fun in the deep end, I came
to the realization that it was a more appropriate environment
for me than the shallow end, which, to that point, had been
the limit of my experience. I was convinced that I needed to
expand my boundaries, and one day I set out in the direction of
the deep end. I must add that this was not without forethought
or preparation, as I had been practicing getting back to the
safety of the pool edge in the shallow end, and after careful
analysis, was sure that my shallow-end experiments would

translate to success in the deep end. After arriving at the deep end, I made the decision to go for it and jumped in. Knowing that discretion is also part of valor, I did ensure I jumped in close to the lifeguard chair, for reasons of my own security and well-being. Immediately after jumping, I sank straight to the bottom. I struggled back to the surface, barely managing to get my head above the water, looking to the lifeguard for help.

Unfortunately, even though I was right under the lifeguard's chair, he did not notice me, as his attention was diverted due to all the other splashers, rule-breaking runners, yelling youngsters, and diving-games noise. I panicked, sank to the bottom again, and continued to repeat this process several times, swallowing pool water and gasping for air, until after what seemed an eternity, I was able to somehow finally make it to the safety of the pool edge. I was clearly shaken but undeterred, and while walking home, I thought about my risky decision and made another, more-practical, quality decision and a promise: I needed swimming lessons, and while I, like everyone else, would have to eventually die, I was going to do my very best to not die by drowning! I discussed this with Mom and Dad, and they agreed. I took swimming lessons, joined the swim team, and even won five medals in the Junior Olympics. Later, that promise to avoid drowning was tested several times during my adventures as a Navy SEAL!

As a youngster, I was very competitive and loved to play sports. Football, basketball, baseball, swimming, track. You name it—I gave it a try, and I was pretty good at all of them. But I quickly learned that being a good player didn't mean we would win the game. To win, obviously, takes **teamwork**. Having a really great player on your team is good, but having a team of good players who are coached and motivated to best utilize their skills and to work together as they are coached has a much better chance of giving their very best effort and winning. My high school football coach, Ron Apperson, was another early influence on me and was a strong advocate of **teamwork**, best effort, and **honesty** with yourself and about your contribution to the team. He convinced me that winning isn't everything, although, winning, of course, should be the goal every time you take the field. You sometimes learn more about yourself and your team from losing. Sometimes you just lose to a better team. But remember: never blame a single teammate for the loss even if he believes it was his fault. It is the team, not an individual, that wins or loses a game. It's also important to always look at the things you did right and those you did wrong as both as a team and an individual. Figure out how to avoid those mistakes the next time you play. That's where the team leader, the coach in this case, is an instrumental catalyst. Albert Einstein once said, "Doing the same thing over and over again and expecting a different result is insanity," which is certainly true when referencing mistakes. As I moved into more competitive arenas and played Division One college football at Navy against recognized national-powerhouse teams, the importance of **teamwork,** coaching styles, skills, and motivation to give best effort became even more apparent.

During my time at the Academy, I was fortunate to have a great group of classmates and upperclassmen and was able to observe and experience leadership, both good and bad, every day; that was another good lesson. When you are in leadership roles, you are always on display and being observed from below as well as by your seniors. I learned that leadership is about building trust and confidence with the junior Midshipmen by being fair, making **good decisions**, and setting clear **boundaries of right and wrong.** I certainly wasn't the perfect Midshipman by any means, but I, naively perhaps, respected and trusted the Senior Midshipmen to do the right thing. That was, unfortunately, not always the case. This was another lesson: people have their own personalities, habits, and agendas, and just because they have been trained and screened to be a good example/leader/citizen does not necessarily mean that will be the outcome. You need to pay attention to those habits in the people you work for and those who work for you. Again, experience is the best teacher, and you often learn more about how "not to do it" rather than good characteristics to emulate.

I would be remiss in not mentioning another great influence on me at the Naval Academy. I was an Oceanography major, and one of my professors, Captain N. G. "Monk" Hendrix, USN (retired), had been a World War II submariner. He eventually had command of his own submarine as well as other high-level command assignments during his thirty-year Naval career. He loved the ocean, earned a Ph.D. in oceanography, and came back to teach at the Naval Academy and commiserate with future naval officers. He was a feisty character and had been an All-American lacrosse player at Navy when he attended. He would invite several of us to his office after hours for "extra instruction (EI)" on his courses but nearly always included talk about being good sailors and good commanders. I think he recognized that those of us he invited were going to be career naval officers, and he wanted to give a little old-school philosophy, learned in combat and in less-than-ideal conditions.

It was a great, if somewhat disorganized, forum, and during these sessions, he would oftentimes toss a lacrosse ball with his stick against a brick wall as he spoke, asked questions and opinions, and told "sea stories." What I learned from him only emphasized what I had already started to recognize—**integrity, team building, and quality decisions** for yourself and your people. He also had a unique command philosophy that he simply stated as "Firm, fair, consistent—train to win the war, and when time and opportunity allow, have some fun, both for yourself and your people."

During my Naval Academy senior year, prior to graduation, I was selected as one of five individuals to go directly to Basic Underwater Demolition School in Coronado, California. If successful, I would then begin my career as a Navy SEAL. The leadership training continued as I went through this very challenging and difficult ordeal (I think that is a fair description). After nearly six months of rigorous training, arduous physical demands, and intense mental self-evaluation challenges, I was one of eleven from an original class of seventy-two to graduate. While only eleven may seem inordinately low, that is a normal attrition rate, and this was, without a doubt, absolutely one of the hardest things I have done in my life. I can't really say how others mentally handled the ordeal, but, for me, it was a simple agreement with myself that I was not going to quit. The instructors, whose job it was to weed out those individuals who did not have the physical or mental stamina—and, just as important, the heart and mindset for the job—may tell me that I was not qualified, but I was not going to quit. One interesting discovery about leadership in making the cut was that it was obvious that the few of us who progressed into the SEAL teams were all highly motivated, very capable individuals. The leadership demands and skills required in dealing with such elite and motivated people and their very complex and varied assignments would be more complicated than anything I had so far observed.

My first fleet assignment as a new Ensign but now, proudly wearing the SEAL warfare trident, was with Underwater Demolition Team 11 (UDT 11). That was the start of a long succession of leadership challenges and learning experiences, and all would emphasize the great importance of **integrity, teamwork, and quality decisions.** I worked with SEALs who had served in Vietnam and were "the experts" in jungle warfare, actual combat situations, and small-group warfighting tactics, and now they worked for me. During this phase of my career, I served in various and escalating leadership assignments from weapons officer, to assistant platoon commander, and then to platoon commander. During this "new guy" period, I used the lessons from previous leadership training and experience and developed my own leadership personality, still observing and learning. But I was now exposed to the importance of Navy middle management—Chief Petty Officers. The Chief Petty Officers, or CPOs, are the experienced, detail-managing, hands-on supervisors for the troops in the command. They reached their professional status through years of experience and positive evaluation by peers and seniors. I worked hard to get to know them and to solicit their advice. That recognition of the importance of these specialized middle managers would continue throughout my career.

SEAL Platoon Commander is, in my view, the most important job a new SEAL officer can have. Platoons, over time, have varied in size from fourteen to sixteen men. The platoon chain of command is Platoon Commander, Assistant Platoon Commander, Master Chief, Senior Chief, Chief, and Squad Leaders. All these leadership positions must be able to operate cohesively but often independently. So, as Platoon Commander, that was my "team," figuratively, from my leadership perception and literally, as the SEAL organization calls them "teams." Team formation and **teamwork** are critical! The Platoon Commander must gain the trust and confidence of the Chief Petty Officers. The relationships between the officers, the Chief Petty Officers, and the troops must be smooth/good/transparent in order to accomplish some very hazardous and very independent missions. To become a good leader, you must understand and show appreciation for members of your team; you must earn their respect for your leadership and especially your cognitive reasoning and ability to make quality decisions without total or accurate information; you must recognize those who excel and encourage those who are struggling. Your reputation as a leader will follow you as you move to new assignments. However, past performance is no guarantee of success, so regardless of what you have done in the past, you will be called upon to form a new team that performs to your standards, and you will be continually observed and judged by your people on your leadership skills. Positive judgment will go a long way toward making the team successful.

As I became more senior, besides being the ultimate team-builder and decision-maker for my group, one of my biggest responsibilities was to teach good leadership to my teams, both by my observable actions and tactful (or not so tactful, if required) advice and direction. I don't know if I was a "natural" leader, but I felt comfortable with the job. I worked hard to engender the trust of those who worked for me as well as with my seniors. I definitely became a better leader with experience and tried to create a "success environment and mindset" for my guys: quality work is much more valuable than the number of hours you work; get it done, but get it done right the first time; if you are struggling, talk to those who have the most experience in the work you are doing; ask questions; demonstrate that you are willing to listen; learn from others even if they work for you. In spite of the fact that you are the "leader," you are not "all-knowing," and if you ever think you are, you're in the wrong job. You also have to realize that not everyone in your team will be onboard with everything you advocate/ direct. You definitely want feedback and input, even dissent, but everyone should know that, once they have given their very solicited advice/opinion, yours is the final decision, and your plan will be executed. Troublemakers often challenge leaders and may try to divide the team. This must not happen, and you cannot let your team become divided. If you are the leader, you must take control and make sure everyone knows who is in charge. In the most severe cases, the troublemaker must be fired or reassigned—but not before you have had a discussion with his friends and supporters about why his methods were not in keeping with the team's best interest.

It's fairly clear, I think, that team building is a constantly changing challenge and that leadership is a very situational issue. Traits/techniques that work in some situations may not be applicable in other situations. Later in my career, I had another unique leadership opportunity, when I deployed to the Arabian Gulf in support of Operation Earnest Will (a U.S.

military effort in 1987 and 1988 to counter Iranian attacks on Kuwaiti-owned oil tankers). My title was Commander, Navy Special Warfare Task Unit, Pacific, and my "at sea" command was a mobile sea-based barge, the *Winbrown II*. One of the assets assigned to my command were helicopter units from the Army's 160th Special Operations Aviation Regiment (Airborne). These fast-mover small helicopters, Little Bird AH-6s, were perfect for interdiction missions and were flown by extraordinarily trained and talented pilots. One pilot took it upon himself, contrary to command regulations and briefings, to see how low and fast he could approach the barge and perform a pop-up maneuver from sea level over the barge—probably just a surge of testosterone without thinking. The barge was protected by a host of protective measures, including 50-caliber machine guns. Since the sailors manning those guns had no idea of the pilot's intentions, only their good sense, intense training recognition, and maybe slow reaction prevented a friendly fire casualty. My leadership personality is generally a calm exterior, and I am a believer, most of the time, in the adage "An angry man loses his credibility and his audience." But this was a situation where a point needed to be dramatically emphasized, and when dealing with people who have great confidence and skills, it is sometimes necessary to remind them in hard language and tone of team and individual standards, assignments, and responsibilities. Having an angry Tasmanian Devil act in reserve can be particularly effective if ever really required.

On September 11, 2001, I was serving as Commander, Special Operations Command Central, essentially in charge of all special-force activities from all services that were involved in the Central Command Area of Responsibility (AOR). The CENTCOM AOR includes the Middle East, central Asia, and parts of Africa. Following the terrorist attacks against our country, we transitioned my headquarters warfighting functions from MacDill AFB, Tampa, Florida, to a forward-deployed Joint Forces Special Operations Component Command center (originally in Uzbekistan and then Mazar Sharif, Afghanistan) in support of Operation Enduring Freedom and the War on Terrorism. This was an extraordinary leadership challenge and included coordinating with the Afghanistan Northern Alliance, which was the only anti-Taliban faction still available in the country, and to solicit them as allies. The Northern Alliance cohesion was tenuous at best; they were in retreat and held only 10% of the northern part of the country. So, the task of preparing them for a full campaign against the Taliban government forces was definitely a complex task. The three central figures were warlords of the alliance from different sects of the Muslim religion (Sunni and Shia) and controlled different areas of the very rugged and mountainous terrain. My biggest challenges were coordinating with these leaders to allow our multinational special forces to use the individual warlord-controlled mountain passes and territories (for a price, of course), building an alliance with them, embedding our forces, and supporting them in a coordinated campaign against the much better- and relatively modern-armed Taliban government forces. They were united in their dislike of the Taliban but not much else. These tribal leaders did not really like each other and would power-play for any advantage in what they could receive from our government and—even more difficult for me—how much effort they would provide in support of the others' efforts. Much has been written and even movies made about these operations, so I won't be repetitive. I will just say that this was certainly a different situation than any I had experienced before, and the normal transparency I would advocate in building my team did not apply across the board here! One interesting item (not really leadership related) was that, just as you see in the movies, the Northern Alliance forces did a lot of celebrating by shooting their weapons into the air, and that is fact. We could never convince them that the law of gravity would bring those bullets back down to Earth at the same deadly velocity, so we ran to find cover during celebrations. The fact that they suffered several casualties in their exuberance did not deter the habit!

So, that is a brief summary of some thoughts on leadership. I mentioned at the beginning that there are a multitude of methods, types, traits, and competencies required to get an organization to move in a desired direction and achieve a goal. I was fortunate in my military service and corporate assignments to encounter a number of unique leadership opportunities and challenges and to watch and learn from some very successful—and some not-so-successful—individuals in their leadership roles. I had great support up and down the chain of command and cannot emphasize enough how much of an impact that can have on success or failure. Another almost immeasurable asset to my successful career was the support I received from home and family. Raising a family is hard in the best of conditions, with two present and vigilant parents. It is particularly hard in the military environment and even harder in a "get up and go at any time of day or night" situation. I just cannot over-stress my appreciation for relief from some of that very important home-tasking while trying to deal with command issues, particularly while deployed. I was extremely fortunate and blessed to have a great companion, partner, and friend for a wife who took on so much more than she could ever have anticipated at the onset of our journey together.

In closing, one leadership recipe does not fit all situations or personnel, but if you focus on complete **integrity** in dealing with people, promote a strong sense of **teamwork**, and analyze the situations to make **quality decisions**, you'll have a good start. Be firm, fair, and consistent—and have some fun!

CHAPTER TWO

VICTORIA CLARKE

★ ★ ★ ★ ★

Victoria "Torie" Clarke is a highly respected communications leader in both the public and private sectors. Her distinguished career includes working as U.S. Assistant Secretary of Defense for Public Affairs, as a senior public relations counselor to Comcast Corporation, and, most recently, as head of Global Corporate Affairs (GCA) for SAP, responsible for building credibility for SAP's vision and strategy with priority audiences. Clarke is currently the host of the successful podcast, "Chatter on Books," that features leading authors in diverse and often provocative topics. She serves as a Senior Advisory Committee Member for the Institute of Politics at Harvard Kennedy School and on the Board of the Rumsfeld Foundation. Clarke is also pursuing her Master's in Social Work to further the development of equine therapy for military veterans with PTSD. A published author, she has been a featured guest on programs ranging from ABC's This Week to The Daily Show with Jon Stewart. Clarke graduated from George Washington University.

★ ★ ★ ★ ★

LEADERSHIP IS NOT WHAT IS DONE *to* a group of people. Leadership is fundamentally what is done *for* each person in that group. Many theories of leadership focus on the leader, emphasizing physical traits such as height or bearing and personality traits such as charisma or energy. Such traits are clearly assets for someone who aspires to lead an organization. But, by focusing on the leader and not the people to be led, this perspective misses the point.

Effective leadership is about forging a conviction among the people in the organization that the aspiring leader cares about each of them and is fundamentally committed to their success over his or her own. A commitment I make to every person I hire is to help them be the very best they can be. That could mean offering professional development and opportunities that go beyond their job description, or anything else that I believe will help them progress as much as possible in their roles and grow along the way. I am a big advocate of the maxim "No discomfort, no growth," as true growth *does* take place outside of your comfort zone. I would make a conscious effort to help people do this. If done in the right way, with the right mentoring, it is a tremendous growing experience for that individual and will give them the confidence and the courage to take on those inevitable challenges they will face.

If at some point I can no longer offer someone opportunities to advance, I will help them find those opportunities elsewhere. While many people resent others poaching their people, I take it as a compliment. It proves that I have helped to develop them and created opportunities for them. It would be selfish of me, and contrary to my values, to keep someone in a position just because he or she is useful to me, while denying them advancement opportunities, wheresoever they may be. As head of Global Corporate Affairs at SAP, a large German software company, I developed a good reputation for hiring terrific people and training and motivating them to be highly functioning professionals who could produce results, manage people, and keep a close eye on the bottom line. Many of my direct reports were hired into other departments. It was good for the people, good for the company, and good for me. One of the best outcomes of my people moving into other parts of the company was that they were advocates for our unique and very forward-leaning approach to communications.

As I look at my own development, there were many people who had a significant impact on me in my early years. The common thread was that all of them were deeply committed to doing quality work. That might be an Irish horse trainer who treated every horse in his care as though it had potential to be a national champion. Or the graphics editor for whom I worked at the now-defunct *Washington Star* who made the paper one of the most engaging publications in the country despite limited resources and stiff competition. In the policy arenas, I was fortunate to work for people like Senator John McCain, Bush 41 and 43, and then U.S. Trade Representative Carla Hills; all of them put country before party and demanded the highest of ethical and professional standards. To work for them, you had to bring your "A" game every day. And they all had a strong desire to do what was best for the people, as they cared deeply about the citizens of this country and, for that matter, for those on their team. I found their approach very motivating. That deep sense of conviction and duty has stayed with me and still motivates me today. I am profoundly driven by my desire to help other people do better, generally, and, specifically, to help people further the general good. For most aspiring leaders, the best and only path to forging such a conviction is to care about each and every member of the team. Some leaders draw boundaries between the work environment and the employee's personal life. While respecting all appropriate privacy issues, I want to know about my team's lives. I want to know about their families, their hobbies, and their personal goals and dreams. I always work hard to make sure they strike a balance between work and home life. Every highly functioning team will have periods where it's all hands on deck, 24/7, pedal to the metal. The ability to step up at those times depends a lot on making sure that is not the case all the time. Anyone working 24/7 all the time will burn out. As an example, the Pentagon is always a busy place, the years immediately after 9/11 particularly crushing. I noticed that leaders at the highest level, including Secretary of Defense Rumsfeld and Chairman of the Joint Chiefs of Staff, Richard Myers always took the time to invite their teams to dinner, to their homes on holidays, or casual gatherings in the Pentagon on holidays. I copied their good example and invited my team and their families to our home in Maryland. Sometimes the events were small and sometimes large. These gatherings communicated clearly and honestly that I cared about our people as people, not just as employees, and getting to know them outside of the work environment was of incalculable value for team building and fostering understanding and trust.

How you lead on a day-to-day basis is very important, and the importance of this simple precept is sometimes overlooked.

Here, one of the most important aspects is consistency, otherwise, the team doesn't know what to do or how to react, since that lack of consistency creates uncertainty. As a result, people pivot to a defensive posture and spend more time focusing on what they think they shouldn't do versus what they should do. Of primary importance here is a consistent framework which is based on a philosophy, strategy, and system that is easily executed by your team. A leader must guide the development of a clear vision and mission for an organization, make sure everyone knows their role and responsibility within that mission, ensure employees have the resources and support they need to execute, and get out of their way. If you have hired the best people, engaged them honestly in the mission at hand, and resourced them, you must let them do their jobs. Micromanaging slows things down, shakes confidence, and demoralizes a workforce.

I worked for the cable television industry in the 1990s. Joe Collins, then the head of Time Warner Cable, was one of the best executives with whom I had the privilege of working. Visiting him once in his Stamford, Connecticut, office, I was struck by how clean his desk was. His outbox had a few items in it; he had a document in front of him that he was reading when I came in, but the rest of the desk was spotless. This was a challenging time for the cable industry, and Time Warner Cable had a lot going on. Acquisitions, regulatory battles, and negotiations with content providers kept a lot of cable people working hard. Thinking about my own desk back home covered with papers and "to do" lists and reading piling up, I said, "Joe, how the heck do you keep this desk so clean?" He smiled, pointed to the offices adjoining his and said, "Why do you think I have all those people?" It's an extreme example, but an important one. Hire good people, and let them do their jobs! By the way, Time Warner had a very dedicated and loyal senior management team thanks to Joe Collins.

Rule number one in facing crises is that you had better be prepared for one. Every leader has an obligation to prepare for the inevitable crises that will occur. To do otherwise is malfeasance, as they are inevitable. Every organization of every size, no matter how well run, will face unexpected challenges. A natural disaster can wipe out a warehouse. An employee's wildly inappropriate YouTube video can spark a viral social media campaign and boycott against a company. Planes can fly into buildings. Training and preparation can lessen the likelihood of some crises, but they will happen. And the best approach is to plan *for* them. Anticipate as many as you can, develop the crisis-management plans to address them, and then know that there will be some you never could have imagined. But if you have the right blueprint, your crisis-management plans will get you through a lot of problems. And throughout this entire time, or *recovery process*, as it is sometimes called, there are two things that are of critical importance. One is to communicate as soon as you can that the crisis is addressed, that there is a plan to move forward. Secondly, don't panic. Convey the plan to your audience, be it customers, citizens, or employees, in a manner which imbues confidence and trust.

If you worked at the Pentagon in the 2000s, you divided time to "before 9/11" and "after 9/11." While few could predict several planes flying into buildings, most knew the likelihood of crises occurring at some time. Like most Defense Secretaries in their early months, Rumsfeld tapped a team to put together a crisis-management plan for the Pentagon. They briefed the Senior Staff, military and civilian, on a Saturday in early spring, 2001. There were binders and wire diagram charts that made your eyes bleed and a few hundred new acronyms. Returning to my office, I told my military assistants that, while I certainly was not the military expert in the building, I thought the plan briefed to us had little chance of success in any crisis. It was complex, confusing, and lacking any sense of who would do what, when, and how in a crisis.

As I was too new at the time to offer a Pentagon-wide alternative plan, I asked my Senior Military Assistant, Army Colonel George Rhynedance, to work on one for the Public Affairs Department, which consisted of 200 people in the building and another 750 worldwide. Rhynedance took a week and came back with a plan that has served as a model for me to use in many different public- and private-sector endeavors in the years since. His plan was beautiful in its simplicity. Its framework: What are our objectives, what is everyone's primary role and responsibility, and how will we communicate with one another? Our objective: develop and communicate the most important information as accurately and quickly as possible. Roles and responsibilities: Who will liaise with military and civilian leadership? Who has sign-off on information and key messages? Who will communicate with Public Affairs employees? Who will work with the White House, State, and CIA? Internal communications: How will we communicate with one another?

When the second plane hit the South Tower of the World Trade Center at 9:02 a.m. on September 11, 2001, most in national security understood immediately the implications.

This was not a random accident but a coordinated attack, probably by known terrorists. Normal interagency procedures were immediately underway, including efforts to determine other threats, get all commercial aircraft on the ground, prevent other attacks, and prepare a response. When American Airlines Flight 77 crashed into the Pentagon at 9:37 and started a large fire, "normal" went out the window. Ground truth information was hard to come by, as leadership at all key agencies, including the White House, was scattered throughout Washington and the country, and many—appropriately—were consumed with helping the injured and those trapped in the wreckage.

While literally thousands of people performed bravely and superbly that day, I was particularly proud of the work of the Pentagon Public Affairs Department, and our efforts were aided greatly by Rhynedance's crisis-management plan. I stayed with Secretary Rumsfeld and then Vice Chairman of the Joint Chiefs Richard Myers throughout the day and evening, developing with them the key messages and information we felt confident sharing. Several times throughout the day, I communicated with my counterparts at the White House, State Department, and CIA to ensure we all had the same information. One of my top deputies, Bryan Whitman, quickly established a press-briefing site approximately a quarter mile from the burning Pentagon, from which I and a few other officials could offer briefings throughout the day, since the media and most personnel had evacuated from the building.

Perhaps the most genius part of the communications plan was the simplest. Like many people and organizations, most of us had become overly reliant on cell phones, contact lists, and key numbers on our desktops. Paper, to many, was seen as antiquated. Again, with little knowledge of what kind of crisis we might face, Rhynedance knew the network vulnerabilities that could stymie communications and worried that we relied too heavily on systems that could be easily compromised in a variety of ways. Sure enough, the chaos of 9/11 everywhere, including the Washington, DC, area, knocked out many systems. Cell service was sporadic to non-existent. Forced to evacuate quickly from their offices, many people did not have key phone numbers or ways to reach critical counterparts in the government. Foreseeing that sort of problem, Rhynedance insisted well before 9/11 that we all keep hard copies of key contacts and multiple phone numbers for each with us at all times. I had copies with me at all times, in my home and in the glove compartment of my car. To this day, I continue this practice and always have hard copies of key contacts with me.

Leaders face challenges. Always have, always will. An effective leader will not only face those challenges but, even more importantly, be vigilant and accept the fact that the environment is changing and that the only constant is change. The biggest challenge leaders face today is the global economic and geopolitical transformation underway and the very high expectations people have—realistic or otherwise. These expectations are fueled by the massive reach and influence of social media and digital communication where, with a few keystrokes, confidence can be restored, or chaos and uncertainty can ensue. A leader today must be acutely aware of this phenomenon or practice, and, quite frankly, suck it up and deal with it. It's not going away. It's here to stay. Leaders often don't want to focus on communication. On more than one occasion, I have heard a leader, official, or executive remark,

"Isn't that your job?" Well, it is, but it is also *their* job as well. The leaders of the organization they represent must be engaged in every aspect of the information environment, including social media. Employees, customers, and citizens expect and deserve to hear from their leaders in an honest and transparent way. They must also be cognizant of the fleeting attention spans which are so prevalent today and be able to explain their mission in a simple sentence or two. As Maxwell D. Taylor, Chairman of the Joint Chiefs of Staff under Kennedy, put it, "If you can't communicate it, you probably don't know what you're trying to accomplish."

Looking back, there are very few things I would have done differently. Many people who have worked with me would probably comment that I should have slowed down, but I always tried to set the example and never asked anyone to work harder than I would. While I was impatient at times, my intense desire to be actively involved and attain our goals drove me. And that desire to be involved and to work hard is exactly what you should do in your leadership journey. Stretch yourself, take on new responsibilities, partner with as many people you can, and simply do it. You will learn as you go, which is the best and only way I ever learned leadership.

To sum up, leadership comes down to your abilities with people. Hire people more talented than you. Make clear your mission and intent. Resource and support them. Stay out of their way, and give them the credit they deserve, privately and publicly. Perhaps most important of all, know that, at the end of the day, you are in charge. Be prepared to take responsibility when things go wrong, because the ultimate responsibility is yours, and yours alone. I wish you all the best, Torie.

CHAPTER THREE

JACOB KASHIWAGI

★ ★ ★ ★ ★

Dr. Jacob Kashiwagi has been the Managing Director at Kashiwagi Solution Model Inc. for five years and the Chairman of the Board for Leadership Society of Arizona for four years. For the last fifteen years, he has been a senior researcher for the Performance Based Studies Research Group (PBSRG). He received his Ph.D. in supply chain management at the Delft University of Technology in the Netherlands, his master's in construction management, and bachelor's in industrial engineering at Arizona State University. As a former professor at Arizona State University, and author of the No-Influence Leadership theory, Dr. Jacob facilitates professional development for businesses, colleges, and high schools. During his time at ASU, Dr. Jacob was one of the highest-rated professors in the School of Engineering. Under his personal mentorship, more than 100 students have completed their education and found leadership positions in various industries. Dr. Jacob has developed the No-Influence Leadership model through more than 1,500 projects across 15 countries, *valued at $4.9 billion, with a 98% success rate, since 2005. His research saves organizations 10–13% on project costs. Dr. Jacob has taught more than 8,000 professionals, 1,500 college students, and 2,500 high school students. He has given hundreds of presentations, educating thousands of service professionals. He has authored 83 academic publications, co-authored 10 books, and is a two-time Amazon Best Selling author of* In Search of Truth *and* No-Influence Mentoring. *In 2020, Dr. Jacob was selected as one of the 40 Under 40 top business leaders by the* Phoenix Business Journal.

★ ★ ★ ★ ★

Since the topic of this book is leadership, the first thing I will delve into is "What is 'leadership,' and how do you define it?" Interestingly, this is something I took a very hard look at during my graduate education at Arizona State University, where I invested a great deal of time and effort researching different ideas and definitions of "leadership." What I envisioned as a relatively simple quest evolved into something else, as the results of my search uncovered hundreds of different definitions of leadership. For some of the definitions, the focus was more on the actions a person demonstrates, whereas others focused more on the position or status in life one had attained and how they had reached that position.

After countless hours of research and reading, I realized the answer had been in front of me all along as I hearkened back to my undergraduate studies in industrial engineering. It was there I was introduced to the man they call the father of modern-day management, Peter Drucker. His definition was,

"The only definition of a leader is someone who has followers."
This definition is simple, concise, and straightforward, which
reflects the way he approached a lot of things. Drucker was
never impressed by the continual advancements and complexity
of the definition of 'leadership' and stated, "Leadership does
matter, of course. But, alas, it is something different from
what is now touted under this label. It has little to do with
'leadership qualities' and even less to do with 'charisma.' It
is mundane, unromantic, and boring. Its essence is performance." The definition of "leadership" is simply someone who
has followers and can produce results. You can imagine that,
with a definition like this, it impacts different types of people
in many different positions. In fact, with this definition, you
almost always need to assume that everyone you meet is a
leader in some form or fashion.

While I didn't realize it at the time, this actually has
helped me in my life, because coming out of high school,
I was the last person anyone thought would be a leader
in any way. I was a 5' 4", 100-pound Japanese kid whom
everyone knew because of my last name (Kashiwagi), which
they couldn't pronounce correctly, and ended coming out
"Kawasaki" or "Squish-a-Froggy" or something crazy. I never
exceled at anything. Moreover, I didn't understand how to
communicate with people very well. I kept to myself and
wasn't comfortable in large groups of people. While there
are specific traits and characteristics that are desirable for
a leader to maximize performance, many of those were not
within me at that time. However, I was very results-driven
and had the confidence and inner drive to focus my time and
energy on just that—getting results. I was certain, or at least

very hopeful, these results would serve as a springboard for me and serve as a beacon of inspiration to others. And, in fact, that did happen. Results begat results, and with each success came renewed confidence and new goals. In just fifteen years, I would become a professor, teach thousands of students, and develop a leadership organization that has helped hundreds of high school students each year. I still find it hard to believe. In retrospect, it was due primarily to the fact that I never felt I had to be a certain way to be a leader. I focused on getting results. I placed no limitations on myself, nor did I feel inadequate in any sense. I just had to be me.

You might have guessed from my definition of a leader that I am firmly in the camp that says that leaders are born, not made, which is a discussion society has struggled with throughout time. I realize it may be discomfiting for some of you to be told that, regardless of how much training and education you go through, you cannot develop into a leader. While you may see this as "bad" news, the "good" news is that *everyone* is born to be a leader—which is an important distinction to bear in mind if you view yourself as a leader. What makes you a leader is not the same thing that makes someone else a leader. The leadership one person exhibits is not the same as someone else exhibits. The type of leadership you have is not something anyone else can possess and is not transferable. This is what makes you valuable and makes every person valued—they possess something that cannot be developed in anyone else but themselves.

Why can't someone be *taught* to lead? As noted above, because everyone is different. Everyone has two things that make them unique—their genetics and their experiences in life. These two things dictate your capability, your capacity, and how you interact with people. No matter how many classes you take in management and leadership, no one can teach you to act like another person or do things in a certain way. You will always have your own way, and it will never be exactly the same as another person.

This naturally brings up the topic of leadership training and its efficacy. If you research the impact of leadership training in the U.S. or elsewhere, you will discover two things. Firstly, companies cannot track their return on investment for leadership training. No one knows the impact or has found a reliable methodology to effectively assess the true impact. Secondly, the leaders in our country and organizations come from a variety of backgrounds. Many come from Ivy League universities and prestigious training programs, with many of the students coming from wealthy and successful families and have what many would refer to as *good genetics*. This begs the question, "Was it the training or the genetics that made them successful?" If it was the training, it stands to reason that the students going to those universities and programs should *all* turn out to be successful and leaders in society, but that is not the case. On the other hand, you also find there are many individuals who never went to college or received training but turned out to be successful and accomplished leaders. Why is that, and what does it mean? To me, it reinforces my point that people are born with their talents and traits, and it is the experience and the results which shape them. Thus, even more important than getting into a good university or training program is to find out who you are and what you do better than anyone else. The more you understand yourself, the more you will put yourself in a situation to succeed and be an effective leader. This is where your true power lies.

As we are all different, all leaders will be different. The characteristics that work for one individual and make that leader successful will not necessarily help make another leader successful. For example, you have people like Abraham Lincoln, whose success was due to traits such as honesty, sincerity, openness to other opinions, and acceptance of all people. Then you have people like Adolf Hitler, who had the exact opposite traits. You also have people like the Dalai Lama, who is very peaceful and quiet, versus someone like Bill Parcells, who was a very vocal football coach and not averse to getting in someone's face. All of these people were renowned leaders, but they led in their own way. To be honest, the people who determine what characteristics an effective leader will have are the followers. Thus, for leaders trying to improve, one of the best things they can do to improve is to observe and watch the reactions of their followers.

While everyone is different and has their own style or characteristics, there are some patterns or general rules on leadership characteristics that are common throughout and can help a leader develop. I was taught this by my father, who is a world-renowned construction-management expert. He was a full professor at Arizona State University and through his work has helped countless individuals and organizations in numerous countries across the globe. He would tell me growing up that his only contribution to the world that he made was a tool he called the Kashiwagi Solution Model (KSM), which evaluates people on their ability to observe reality. The KSM operates on a spectrum—on one end you have someone who understands 100% of all information, and, on the other end, you have someone who comprehends almost nothing. Thus, it takes the extreme, while minimizing the amount of information, to identify who they are. For example, if you had two pencils that were exactly the same except that one had a small scratch on the side, you would need to do a thorough inspection of both pencils to figure out why they are different. If you were looking at them from a distance, you might not even know they were different. It's the same with people. The more similar they are, the more information you need to tell them apart, but if you take the extremes, you can quickly identify who they are. Consequently, by taking the extreme, you can understand the general idea of what makes them different with minimal information.

I used this model to understand the difference between leaders. Regardless of what type of leader they are, there are leaders who understand more of reality and leaders who understand less of reality. By understanding the extremes, we can quickly understand leadership types and also what type of characteristics we need to become that type of leader. The KSM model is very easy to understand and basically distinguishes the characteristics of Type A and Type C leaders. Type A leaders are those who have more information and a greater grasp on the situation. Type C leaders are the reverse of this—often taking that leap of faith based on intuition or gut feeling, with concordant emotional appeals.

The Type A leaders are more likely to have the following characteristics:

1. See further into the future
2. Are less stressed and worried
3. Believe less in chance and luck
4. Are more accountable for themselves
5. Think of others more
6. Try to control other people less
7. Are less emotional
8. Utilize the strength of others more
9. Make fewer decisions and take fewer risks

The Type C leaders are more likely to have the following characteristics:

1. Think short term
2. Are more stressed and worried
3. Believe in chance and luck
4. Are less accountable
5. Think more of themselves
6. Try to control others more
7. Want to have more excitement and thrills in their life
8. Want to take risks and make decisions

While most of you reading this book will probably want to be more like a Type A leader, there are two important characteristics to note. First, they realize they don't know everything, which makes them capable of learning very quickly because they are good listeners, more receptive to accepting help, and utilizing the strengths of others. Understanding that no one can do anything on their own, they more readily utilize the expertise of everyone around them versus trying to be the expert in everything. As I always tell my students, there are hundreds of people looking for jobs every day but very few people who know how to utilize the people around them to do something of value. The world needs people who know how to use other people to do something great.

Secondly, Type A leaders have the ability to change. The ability to improve yourself each day is a capability that must be practiced in order to develop it. This is one of the most overlooked skills today. This skill is needed to change anything about you. It could be changing your routine or changing what you eat, how you do your work, etc. Leaders who understand this start to develop this skill from a young age. It is what enables them to advance more quickly than other people. While every leader will not be 100% Type A or 100% Type C, they will always be somewhere in between. I encourage you to figure out what you would like and what works best for you in various scenarios; then work toward developing the right characteristics.

Over the course of my career, there are several people I have admired and who have helped me along the way, the first being my father. My father is a world-renowned expert in the delivery of construction and services. He was a full professor at Arizona State University, Fulbright Scholar, and the creator of a delivery system (the Best Value Approach) that the Netherlands trains all of their professional consultants in. He also developed one of the longest-lasting construction-research groups (The Performance Based Studies Research Group) and has written more than 350 journal articles and numerous books. I observed how my father worked, his perspective on issues, and what he desired in life. I quickly realized two things: the first was that I am much like him, and the second was that not many people ever understand or are exposed to what it takes to be an expert in something. I made the decision when I was young to work with my dad to gain this experience.

I remember that, when I first started working with him, I would work what seemed like all day and night. We would have an incredibly structured routine. Every day, we would wake up at 4:30 a.m. to exercise, get to work by 7:00 a.m., and then work all day. I would get a break when I needed to go to my undergraduate classes, but then I would go right back to work with him, and we would often work to 10:00 p.m. or 12:00 midnight. No matter how late we worked, we would be right back at it the next day at 4:30 a.m. I also observed how much my father wrote. He is not naturally a good writer, but, regardless of how many research projects he was undertaking, how much he was traveling, how many people he was meeting with, and how many classes he was teaching, he always found time to write. I asked him many times, "Why write so much, especially since most of your writing will never be read by anyone?" He told me that if you can't write it down, then you don't understand it. In order to write, you must see the solution, be able to explain it simply, and know the value it has to others. Even if no one reads it, it ensures that you understand, as writing develops you.

These are just a few of the many other lessons I learned in working with my father, with whom I have worked for more than 20 years now and continue to work with. While many people thought that I worked with him so closely because I was his son—or perhaps because I had no other options—that is not the reason. The real reason I have worked with my father is because I realized he is an expert and is incredibly successful. To become an expert, you have to work with one. His mentorship has been of incalculable value, and I am thankful for it. Unfortunately, this is something many young people are not taught today, nor do they appreciate how much they can learn from older generations who have been successful and whom they should respect.

This has led me to my current mission, which is to aid in the development of the younger generation. While teaching at Arizona State University, I taught an honors class that was filled with the top 10% of students at the university from all the different colleges. Even though I wasn't paid to teach—I was a research professor—I taught that class because I cared about the students. As I did so, I noticed a major problem. Even though I was working with the top 10% of students, they still did not know how they would add value to society and had difficulty getting to sleep at night. After doing some research, I discovered the issue they all had in common. The common thread was that, in their youth or formative years, they were inundated with so much information that it forced their minds to continually process and think, so much so that they literally could not shut it off. It confused them to the point that they didn't know what they enjoyed, how they could apply any of the information, or even relax, for that matter. It dawned on me that one person could not make a big enough impact to change anything. A different approach was required. I subsequently employed two Ph.D. students, mentored them, coached them, and helped them develop a non-profit startup organization that would go out and educate not only the youth but also parents on the change that needs to occur to develop better students. This non-profit has now been running for four years, and it has impacted more than 2,400 students and 2,000 parents. This organization will only get larger and will continue to spread this idea. I found that a leader impacts society not by doing something themselves, but by being able to utilize and align the people and resources around them.

Looking back, you would never have thought I could become the person I am today. If you knew me when I was a freshman in high school, you would have thought that I wasn't cut out to be a leader. If you talked to me, you would have noticed that I had no social skills, especially when talking with girls. You may have thought I was a typical Asian-American who was small and geeky—but super smart and in all the advanced classes—but you would have been wrong. You would eventually find out I was not in any advanced or honors classes and that I didn't do well in the basic courses I was enrolled in. When it came to math, I really had issues. On top of that, I didn't really have a group of friends in high school. I had drifted apart from my group of friends in junior high school, so I was kind of a loner. On the surface, none of this bothered me, because I didn't realize this when I was a freshman—at least not to this extent. In my mind, I thought I was a superstar! It was like I had one of those mirrors that reflects back what you want to see instead of what is actually there.

This set the stage for when I found the biggest challenge that all leaders must face—themselves. All leaders have a defining moment in their life when they figure out who they are and realize they were wrong about themselves. At this point, they see all their flaws, realize how many mistakes they have made, how inadequate they are in moving forward with their life, and think they don't even have a chance at success. My father had a sign in his office that said, "I was so far behind I thought I was first." Later, during my high school career, I related to this quote. Up until high school, I thought I was awesome! I thought I was the best and that I was so far ahead, but my eyes were opened. I started to realize that I was not ahead of everyone—I was just really far behind!

This challenge will come to every leader—no matter if you are really gifted or if you are a small Japanese boy with no gifts. The reason is that no one is perfect or can do everything perfectly. There is always going to be someone better than you at something. You also live with yourself, so you will notice everything you do wrong, unlike with others, where you see only the perfect side of them. Eventually your eyes will open to how "bad," "imperfect," and "incapable" you are. The key is how you deal with this when you figure it out. Will you accept it, and will it give you more motivation to work harder and be better? Will this help you understand yourself and give you information to develop yourself as you move into the future? Will it make you humble and help you realize the value of everyone? Or will it cause you to be more insecure and fearful? Will it zap your energy and destroy your desire to be great? Will it cause you to become apathetic toward the world around you and develop in yourself a culture of laziness? Will you deny it and become bitter about the unfairness in life?

Whichever way you take when the challenge comes will be right for you. However, I noticed that one thing that distinguishes leaders who are more observant is that this challenge usually makes them stronger and humbler. It is what allows them to utilize the resources around them most efficiently to produce something of value to society.

We all have obstacles to overcome, and I was no exception. One of my first was overcoming a speech impediment. I was not able to pronounce my "t" and "r" sounds and went to speech therapy throughout fourth grade. Because of this, I was sometimes made fun of, as many people couldn't understand what I was saying. Throw in the fact that I was Japanese—in environments where there was only a handful of Asians—and the fact that my family moved seven times before I was fifteen years old, and you'll understand that I was constantly on the defensive. After I graduated with my master's, I was kicked out of my Ph.D. program due to my father being a professor in the department. And while trying to develop my high school curriculum, I faced resistance from many people within my own research group and had difficulty obtaining funding and securing resources. Consequently, I became even more defensive, carrying that chip on my shoulder.

As I grew, developed, and experienced small measures of success, it finally dawned on me that the biggest obstacle to success was someone I saw in the mirror every day—myself. I always thought it was other people, not enough opportunity, or not enough funding keeping me from being more than I was. It wasn't until I was around thirty that I realized, in order to be successful, I needed to accept reality, understand people, and understand what is possible. I realized my speech impediment wasn't an issue—it was my lack of self-confidence that caused people to pick on me. It wasn't being Asian that caused me to be seen as an outcast—it was my insecurity that caused me to be defensive and prideful and not to fit in. It wasn't being my dad's son that got me kicked out of my program—it was my feeling of entitlement and lack of accountability that prevented me from making it, and the list goes on. Funding and resources were an issue only because I didn't really have anything of value developed. Once we developed something that worked and had value that we could explain, funding was no longer an issue.

Along the way, you will make mistakes. That is how you learn. However, I attribute one of the problems with many leaders to what I call "the John Wayne syndrome," i.e., the characterization of a leader being in full command of the situation, knowing all, and always coming to the rescue—just like in the movies. Unfortunately, life does not imitate art in this respect, although many people believe that it does. This results in many leaders making the following mistakes:

1. Trying to do more instead of delegating tasks
2. Equating their value with doing the work
3. Spending time trying to change people
4. Spending too much time acquiring technical information as a means to become the "expert"
5. Not valuing other people enough
6. Spending more time on day-to-day activities versus developing a long-term vision

These mistakes imply that a leader's value diminishes if they don't work enough. Throughout time, the leader has never been the technical expert. It has always been more important for the leader to be able to *utilize expertise* than to *be the expert.* This is the same now, as it is more important for the leader to have vision and align the right resources in the right places to move toward it. Without this taking place, more and more, the leader gets dragged into the day-to-day operations of the business to "fix things," with less time spent on strategy and planning—often to the detriment of an organization.

In my classroom and at the Leadership Society of Arizona, one topic that comes up frequently is if there is a one-size-fits-all type of leadership. As you probably surmised, due to my views on leadership, I definitely do not believe that is the case, as no two people can have the exact same style of leadership. Each will have something a little different, depending on who they are. As for my specific leadership philosophy, I call it the No-Influence Leadership model. The core belief with this model is that a person has no impact, influence, or control over other individuals. Thus, you must lead by accurately identifying who people are, what they naturally do, and utilizing their strengths to help the organization or cause. The leader should not be trying to change an individual from who they are into something else—that will only minimize direction, training, education, and communication. In fact, the more you have to interact, the more it reinforces the point that you, as the leader, did not find the right person or people. In this model, the follower is always right. Instead of the follower listening to the leader and doing what they say, the leader must listen and adjust according to input from the followers.

This model was developed from ideas from other great leaders that I felt were accurate as I went through my education. A couple of them are as follows:

1. Bruce Lee—He believed that success was found by following what he called the law of harmony. This meant never to go against nature but always to follow it. Thus, if a person is punching you, instead of trying to block him, you adjust your movement to go around him, and then use his momentum to allow him to destroy himself. Thus, I do not believe going against what people naturally do is beneficial. Instead, we must follow their natural movement; the less they have to change, the more efficient they will be.

2. W. Edwards Deming—He identified that anything an organization does to motivate, influence, or change an individual doesn't work. The best thing a leader can do is observe what is happening and track the current conditions through measurement. He identified that, while most organizations think the issues come from an individual, almost every issue is caused by the process and organization more than by the actual employee.

3. Jim Collins—He identified that the best business leaders would concentrate on finding expert people and placing them in the right slot in the organization. That alignment of the individual's strength is what enables organizations to grow and perform.

One of the takeaways I am sure you are looking to get from my chapter is what recommendations I have for someone who is looking to become a leader or further develop their leadership. Here, my advice is straightforward and as follows:

1. **Be patient with yourself.** Developing anything that will last a lifetime and is valuable takes time, so don't be in a rush. Enjoy your life. Don't worry if it seems that other people are advancing more quickly than yourself. This life is definitely not a sprint, and it is very deceiving sometimes as you try to identify what will actually help you.

2. **Find a mentor.** Life is always easier when you learn from experienced people instead of trying to do everything on your own. Make sure this person is older than you. Make sure you talk to this person about everything that you are doing. The more you use a mentor, the easier your life will be, and the fewer mistakes you will make.

3. **Accept compliments.** Don't think people are telling you things just to be nice or that they are trying to build you up. If someone says you did a great job, take it at face value, and accept it. When I was younger, I didn't do this, and I was always thinking that I didn't really do anything very well. I only later realized that the compliments I would get were real and that they were feedback for me to learn more about myself.

4. **Have faith.** Have faith in yourself. Believe in what you are about, and that you are capable of doing anything if you put your mind to it and work for it. If you have a dream, go for it, because there is a reason that you have it.

5. **Be objective.** When assessing something or making decisions, ensure that you not only have solid

information but that you are non-biased when making decisions for the organization. The more devoid your decisions are from bias and emotion, the greater the chance that you will make a good decision. The more bias and emotion enter the equation, the more you impair your judgment and risk making a bad decision.

When I look at life and people, I realize that people don't change much. Looking at my own life and my goals, they have not really changed very much. When I was younger, my goals were always focused on self-improvement and understanding why things happen. I was never a detail-oriented person; I wanted a greater vision of life. I wanted to know why I was who I was, why something happened to me, and why people did what they would do. I would also spend a lot of time with religious activities and debating with my religious leaders on why they believed what they believed. During my high school years, I spent a lot of time in speech and debate. I focused on activities and classes in school that identified why things would happen. I joined clubs that helped me to understand what people were thinking. I also spent a lot of time as I went through my college career volunteering at a place with a lot of older and more-experienced individuals. I always had an affinity for talking with older people and asking them about their life, what they had gone through, and their views on it. As I get older, my goals are still the same. I am even more focused on developing myself. I work on being a nicer, more service-oriented person. I have a greater vision of life now; I look for information that confirms it and reminds me of the purpose of life. I have found as I get older and know more, my goal has become more about helping others who are trying to figure it out and to make a difference in their lives. And above all, in everything I do, large or small, I ensure that I add value.

CHAPTER FOUR

CARL H. SHARPERSON, JR.

★ ★ ★ ★ ★

"Quitters Never Win. Winners Never Quit."

Carl Sharperson, Jr. is a Leadership Innovation Strategist, speaker, author, and coach. He specializes in taking leaders from mediocre to maximizing their potential in work and personal life. He transforms his audience and coaching clients through his proprietary Sharp Leadership coaching process as well as drawing from his unique experiences in the military, Corporate America, and entrepreneurship. A graduate of the United States Naval Academy and a former United States Marine Corps pilot with a BS in Engineering, Carl documented those experiences in his book Sharp Leadership: Overcome Adversity to Lead With Authenticity, *which is a life-changing book. Following his service, he went on to hold a number of senior sales and operational positions with Frito Lay, Procter & Gamble, and Colgate Palmolive. In fact, he was the Vice President of Manufacturing for an international sports company when he felt the tug toward entrepreneurship.*

He then launched Sharperson's Executive Leadership in 2000, where he has worked with executives at a diverse range of companies, including: Harley Davidson, BMW, University of North Carolina, and Chick-fil-A, just to name a few. As a speaker, Carl travels nationally; he was trained by the Center for Creative Leadership in Greensboro, North Carolina, as an adjunct trainer, where he specialized in executive coaching, leadership, and organizational development. Carl recognizes the value of giving back and works on several community- and faith-based initiatives, serving as a mentor and a resource to maximize the potential of youth today. Carl and his wife make their home in upstate South Carolina, and they are the proud parents of a son and a daughter.

★ ★ ★ ★ ★

THERE ARE MANY DEFINITIONS OF "LEADERSHIP." Everyone has their own definition or understanding of what constitutes effective "leadership." From my perspective, effective leadership is getting people to follow you; as you grow and develop them, it should be done in such a manner that they can operate on their own and become self-reliant in your absence.

One of the age-old questions is whether leaders are born or made. My take is 10% of what makes an effective leader is something you are born with, and the remaining 90% is predicated on your experience. During your formative years and later, your leadership is cultivated by your environment—the norms in your household when you grew up; the people you associated with and learned from in various environments, such as teachers, coaches, and individuals in the business world;

and, in my situation, in the military. To learn and understand real leadership, it has to be seen, experienced, nurtured, and developed. You can augment your life experience with books, conferences, podcasts, and various other things, as leadership is a continuum. You are always learning and calibrating your leadership skills and your style.

When looking at the characteristics required for someone to be an effective leader, integrity is first and foremost. Integrity is not optional—it is mandatory. A leader should always speak the truth and seek the truth. An effective leader takes care of his or her people, builds relationships, is an effective communicator, all the while imbuing trust and developing a better understanding of each member of the team. Consistency is an important aspect, otherwise, you send mixed messages to the team, which causes confusion and uncertainty as to what they should do and even how they should respond. Effective leaders set the example—their actions mirror their words by walking the talk and never asking someone to do something they wouldn't do. Humility is a desirable trait for effective leaders, who understand that they don't know everything and are open to feedback and new and different ways of doing things. One of my favorite questions to my team was "I am not sure what to do. What do you recommend?" By asking them to be part of the solution, their active involvement and your willingness to listen foster an environment of trust and transparency.

When I look back on the people who influenced me and helped shape me, my parents were first and foremost. My mother and father had a profound impact on me and were a source of inspiration and learning. They set the standard, as, at all times, their actions were consistent with the values they espoused. This reinforced, to me, the need to ensure that my actions were consistent with my spoken word and to walk the talk, so to speak. My head football coach in high school, Hal Sparks, also had a huge impact on me and still does to this day. He is an amazing person, and his life story would make a great movie. I vividly recall the first day of football practice, when he gathered us together and emphasized that once we went out and practiced, he expected us to stay on the team the entire season. As Coach Sparks said that day, "If you quit this team, then you will quit other commitments in your life. You may quit school, your wife, children, and job." That simple statement hit me like a bolt of lightning. I vowed then and there to stay with the team, no matter what, to carry forward in life with the same mindset, and to live that mantra.

The leaders I met and observed at the United States Naval Academy and in the Marine Corps had a significant impact on my leadership development, and it was there that my core leadership values were reinforced. There is no substitute for that day-to-day experience with leaders as you observe, listen, and learn by their example. It is without a doubt the best way to learn leadership. After my service in the military, I was blessed with the opportunity to work with some outstanding people at Procter & Gamble, where the diversity of personnel, opinions, and leadership styles helped me to further hone my leadership skills.

While I did not appreciate it at the time, the experience of integrating school systems in both junior high and high school was a valuable learning experience as well. Needless to say, there were challenges and opportunities, with the environment presenting circumstances and obstacles that I had to deal with, day in and day out, as racial tensions were high at the time. This was uncharted territory for me—and for others, for that matter—and, in hindsight, it helped condition me and made me stronger. Rather than respond to every insult or derogatory word hurled at me—if I had done so, I would have been arguing and fighting all the time—I took the high road and chose not to respond, which is a form of passive resistance. Instead, I let my actions speak for themselves as I strove to set an example that would foster respect, loyalty, and trust based on the quality of my achievements—not the color of my skin. It took a tremendous amount of restraint and discipline, but, over time, walls came down, barriers were removed, and lines of communication were opened. Mutual respect, trust, and even love were established as we began to realize we are all in this together, we all want the same things in life, and that winning or losing our strength of purpose and potential would be realized only if we worked together.

Over the course of my career, being in a leadership position presented a number of challenges, and, as I point out in my book *Sharp Leadership*, the 80/20 rule or "Pareto Principle" often comes into play. When I say, "comes into play," I would estimate that 80% of the people I worked with or observed in leadership positions were not equipped for leadership and were not effective. These mismatches had numerous adverse consequences. Many of the consequences fall into a category I like to refer to as a "spillover effect," which is something that occurred to me when taking on new responsibilities and positions. More often than not, I had to overcome the spillover or collateral damage that occurred due to the dysfunctional leadership style of my predecessor. Overcoming this previous culture required transparency and humility, ensuring my actions mirrored my values, being consistent and fair with all, and getting to know and understand each person, including their strengths and weaknesses. By taking this approach, which was something that had been drilled and instilled into me, I was able to gain trust and re-instill confidence and *esprit de corps* in the team.

On a more macro basis, another challenge I encountered was having to lead in an environment where the culture does not align with its values—or even your own, for that matter. This presents not only challenges but opportunities as well. In many instances, I was able to be an agent of change for the organization by continually emphasizing the importance of ensuring that your actions and decisions were consistent with your values and goals. On the operational side of things, the 80/20 rule also came into play. You cannot focus on everything and solve each and every issue. Ultimately, if you prioritize and take care of the top 20% of the problems or issues facing you, it facilitates your ability to later deal with the other 80% of the less-important issues.

Everyone makes mistakes, and, when you are in a leadership position, the impact is more widespread. It impacts not only the team and their co-workers but the company as well, since shortfalls in leadership can cascade and have a negative impact in many other areas, such as morale and productivity. Looking back at the mistakes most leaders make, ineffective communication ranks very highly. By "communication," I mean not only conveying information in an articulate and concise manner but also *simply listening*. It always baffled me why someone would come onboard or be transferred into a new leadership position and automatically assume they knew best, in spite of the fact that the people reporting to the leader had a breadth and depth of experience. These people are a valuable resource—they run things on a day-to-day basis—and to arbitrarily dismiss or ignore their advice without a candid two-way exchange of information sets the stage for mediocrity and, possibly, even failure. The reasons for someone in a leadership position doing this, based on my experience and observation, usually boiled down to the leader being arrogant, insecure, a bad fit for the position, or a combination of these circumstances.

Another area is integrity, which can cover an entire litany of issues and behavior. One of these behaviors is not being honest and forthright. As noted earlier, it is important to seek the truth and speak the truth. A leader who disregards this basic tenet is compromised from the start. Another is a lack of accountability, which goes both ways. A good leader holds his or her team accountable, empowers them, and supports them. When problems occur, the focus should be on finding a solution, not casting blame. When the latter occurs, and messenger shooting becomes SOP (standard operating procedure), it results in a lack of trust, as the team knows the leader does not have their back. Their *modus operandi* changes, as the focus is more on not what they did right but what they could be blamed for, which immediately puts them in a defensive, non-proactive posture.

I have often been asked what my leadership style is. My standard response was that, while the core principles need to be there, it depends on the individual and the circumstances, as there is no one-size-fits-all. However, throughout my career,

I always strove to be inclusive, aware, and adaptable. By being inclusive, I made it a point to devote a great deal of time to team building and to create events that enabled the team to better know and understand each other. There are various ways to do this, and I was able to draw from my sports and military background to create events and scenarios to make this happen.

Awareness was an important factor in communication and socialization. I made it a point to get out from behind my desk and interact with my team as much as possible. I would solicit their input, ask what they thought about something, and inquire about their families. On the personal front, many of them had loved ones and families, and what happens in one area spills over to another. I created gatherings outside of work so that their families and loved ones could get to know each other—and me, for that matter. Simply knowing more about the other person and what they are about or what they may be going through helped improve communication and gave me a better understanding of how to work with them. On the matter of adaptability, as I mentioned earlier, there is no one-size-fits-all. I always made it a point to be a situational leader, basing my response on the circumstances and personnel on hand.

One technique I found to be successful was asking a simple question, such as, "What's on your mind?" By doing this, you will develop a more in-depth understanding as to what is going on with them and what may be hampering their performance. It could even be a personal issue, and you have to bear in mind that everyone has both a professional life and a personal life, with spillover from one affecting the other. As I mentioned above, I would strive to practice situational leadership and adapt as needed, based both on the circumstances and the team member, understanding that different people are motivated differently.

For example, with a football team, one member may be motivated by the coach getting on to them, even yelling at them, as a means to spur them on further. Just as one person may respond to this attention favorably, another person may not and may find it demoralizing. This is why it is so important to get to know your people, what makes them tick, what their strengths are, and what their weaknesses are. As a leader you also need to be vulnerable. While this may sound a bit odd, your team needs to know that you need and value their advice and their effort. Don't be afraid to say, "I don't know," "I need your help," or "What do you think?" People have a natural tendency to be wanted and to be a part of something. These actions are consistent with these desires.

During my formative years, my goal was to become a professional athlete, and, after a time, it morphed into the desire to be a coach and a leader. I was always fiercely determined and had the will to succeed, never to quit, and always to do my best. Over time I learned what was really important were the relationships that were formed and what you learned from those relationships. When possible, I made it a point to try to give back and be a giver, as opposed to a taker. If you take care of your relationships, never quit, and always do your best, the money and material things are made possible. Your mind is the most powerful thing you have. You have to stay positive and believe in yourself, those around you, and in your mission—you must have faith. I am a man of faith and have always found comfort in reading the word of God. This belief helped to buttress both the physical and mental aspects of leadership, which kept me balanced. I always made it a point to look forward, not in the rearview mirror, and still see myself very much as a "work in progress," constantly learning and evolving. You also need to have a short memory, put things behind you, and move on—taking all that baggage with you will slow you down.

As a means to hone my leadership skills, I have always tried to broaden my views and secure additional insight. I listen to tapes, go to seminars, and try to learn from the best—i.e., someone who has been there and done that—as opposed to a theoretical or textbook approach. This information would do one of two things. It would either reinforce that I was adhering to best practices, or it would give me further insight and ideas on how to approach different situations. In those instances, it was nuanced, but sometimes the smallest thing can make the biggest difference. I always kept an open mind in trying to improve and adapt by learning from these leaders.

There is a lot of money and time spent on leadership training, which is a big business. However, I would submit that formal training, per se, merely augments what is the most effective means of learning, which is hands-on, real-world experience. This underscores the importance of associating with the right people and the right organizations, including a mentor, where you get real-world experience that will translate to practical and effective results throughout your career. The effectiveness of leadership training depends on a number of things, such as the method, the motivation for learning, and having a student who is present and who accepts and understands the message.

But all of this is for naught if you do not have an organization with a culture that sustains this by adopting and implementing best practices—the values and principles central to effective leadership. Sadly, this is not the case, as in most instances, there is no ongoing reinforcement once the training session is over. While it is difficult to quantify the effectiveness or rate of return when it comes to leadership training, I would estimate that leadership training is effective in less than 20% of the cases, with a concordant increase if the organization supports the initiative on an ongoing basis, all the while maintaining a culture which is trusting and conducive to the learning and growing which must take place.

As I mentioned earlier, I still consider myself a "work in progress," so I am continually growing and developing. However, throughout my career, there have been certain principles and traits which I consider inviolate and are central to what I am about. First and foremost is my faith, which is the faith I have in the Lord, the faith I have in my family, and the faith they have in me. Overcoming brain surgery early in my civilian career and, several years later, successfully battling cancer would not have been possible without my faith in God and family. This was the rock which enabled me to have the fortitude and mindset to weather those storms. Secondly, be a person of integrity, with actions that match your words, being truthful and transparent at all times. Thirdly, never give up, and have the resiliency, courage, and strength of conviction to handle whatever comes your way. Fourthly, never lose the ability to empathize with other people, see their point of view, understand what they are about, and connect with them. Last, but not least, maintain a sense of balance and ensure that you spend enough time in all areas of your life so that one does not overshadow another.

In closing, I would like to thank you for taking the time to read this. I hope you were able to glean not only some useful information but also a dose of inspiration. Remember, it's not about you but about *what you are*. Be blessed, Carl.

"It is not what you call me that is important,
but what I answer to."

CHAPTER FIVE

CHRIS MOLINA

★ ★ ★ ★ ★

Hi, there! My name is Chris Molina, and I am the recipient of the 2020 NAMCA College Speaker of the Year Award (National Association for Masterminds & Co-curricular Advancement), an Amazon Best-Selling author of I'm in a Leadership Role. Now What? The Student Edition, *a podcaster on the Professional by Choice Podcast and the How'd You Meet? podcast, a Personal Development Coach, a United States Marine Corps Veteran (serving seven years on Active Duty), a Purdue University Alum, and a Leadership Literacy Expert. More than anything, I'm a father (#GirlDad), a husband, a son, a brother, and an East Chicago, Indiana, native. Most notable for you is probably my time in the Marine Corps and my self-published book on Leadership. But, as you'll read, my leadership literacy has been molded by* all *of my experiences. The Marine Corps gave me a rock-solid foundation for leadership. John Deere taught me what true leadership looks like in the civilian world. Purdue University bridged the gap between the two.*

I say this humbly, but truthfully: What you read from
me is the total opposite of lofty rhetoric filled with fluff
and reverie. I'm solely interested in the complexities of
leadership. Nothing more, nothing less.

★ ★ ★ ★ ★

First of all, thank you for taking the time to read
this and take in my views on leadership. While there are many
definitions of "leadership" out there, to me it is pretty simple
stuff—leadership is influence. If you have ever influenced someone
else, personally or professionally, then you have practiced leadership. Your influence may have had the desired effect, or it may
not have—that's on you. However, understanding the essence of
leadership and best practices will provide you with constancy and
make you a better leader, providing you have the right mindset,
and you invest time and effort to develop and improve.

You have undoubtedly been asked or been involved in discussions about whether leaders are born or if they are made.
When I hear this question, I sometimes reply with "Is a talented mathematician born or made? Is a skilled editor born or
made? Is a scientist born or made?" I view this question about
leadership in the same context as it would apply to anything
else. I enjoy debate on the topic, which in philosophical terms
is called "innate traits vs. acquired traits." This is something I
love studying, and I could write a few thousand words just on
this topic alone. However, I have only one chapter, and, in the
interest of brevity and empathy for the reader who despises
verboseness, I will lean toward brevity.

While the difference between two individuals (one is a
great leader, and the other is mediocre) can be caused by

a genetic or an environmental difference between them, the development of any trait in an individual depends on both genes *and* environment. Every aspect of development, including learning, must first be available to us by our DNA. Conversely, countless aspects of the environment are required at each stage of our lives to keep development on its normal course. If we can agree that leadership is something we can learn and develop, similar to any other academic study, then the answer is both—leaders are both born and are made. It is the combination of nature and nurture which shapes and determines someone's leadership skills, with nurture having the predominant influence. Notwithstanding the importance of your genes or nature, I think we would all agree that we can remove the term "natural-born leader" from our lexicon. There is no such thing.

If you were to look at the characteristics required for someone to be an effective leader, the first one that comes to mind is adaptability. Why is adaptability important? Because all of us are different, and each person needs to be led in a different way. What works for one person or in one instance will not necessarily work in another. It is not strictly plug-and-play as there is no one-size-fits-all leadership. Robert Burns told us that "The best-laid plans of mice and men often go awry." This is abundantly clear to anyone who has held a leadership position—we need to adapt to each situation and also each individual we encounter. Always remember that rigidity is the enemy of good leadership, and you don't always need to be the perfect leader that you imagine, but you do need to be flexible enough to be the leader your group needs.

The next characteristic that comes to mind is the need to be an effective communicator. If you are a poor communicator, chances are you are also a subpar leader, since if you can't properly articulate the mission and convey what needs to be done, nothing will get done well. The desirability and importance of this characteristic looms larger than ever, for myriad reasons. In a book called *Alone Together*, MIT social psychologist Sherry Turkle makes the case that people today are so used to text-based communication, where they have time to gather their thoughts and plan precisely what to say and how to say it, that they are losing their ability to have spontaneous conversations. She argues that the muscles in our brain that assist us with spontaneous conversation are getting less exercise in this text- and email-filled world, so our skills are declining. I agree, because I've witnessed this difference when I speak to people of different generations. I've also observed that the diminishing ability to have effective, spontaneous conversations also affects overall communication. (And then throw in an extraordinary amount of quarantining and social distancing due to COVID-19, and we have a generation of budding leaders who don't have the necessary developmental experiences that all effective communicators have.)

Many individuals in leadership positions are not effective communicators, and when you have ineffective communication combined with a misconception many people have and a trap they fall into, you have all the makings of a disastrous leadership experience. That trap is what I call "the fallacy of competence." Many people start off with the concept that the best way to start proving their ability to be a good leader to their subordinates, peers, or boss is by displaying their competence, expertise, or talent and proving who is in charge. They strive to show everyone they have the necessary skills to make the right decisions, tout their credentials—academic or otherwise—and want to be seen as in charge and taking command. This is almost always accompanied by a large dose of positional authority, bereft of any real understanding of what your team is about, what makes them tick, and how best to lead them. This is the wrong approach to take. Proving your competence is important for leaders, but not initially. Studies show that people's first concerns are about whether you're concerned about their interests, about whether you're warm, and about whether you're caring—not your competence.

The third characteristic is decisiveness, the importance of which was reinforced to me during my time on active duty in the Marine Corps. Simply stated, it means being able to make good decisions in a timely manner. While the definition isn't complicated or convoluted, it does entail a number of things that have to be considered and accomplished. You have to get all of the facts, weigh them against each other, and also gauge the accuracy of the information. You need to be objective and maintain your composure throughout the process. At the right time, you arrive at a sound decision and then announce it in a clear, firm, and professional manner. Sounds like simple stuff, right? Well, it is, and it isn't, and, unfortunately, this ability is wanting in many leaders. While there are many factors that contribute to their inability to be decisive, the single biggest issue is what I referred to firstly—adaptability. In many instances, these leaders are not able to adapt their style and the process to fit the circumstances and the personnel. This can be due to a number of issues such as rigidity, confirmation bias, fear, insecurity, or the inability to communicate (which goes both ways, I might add).

The importance of adaptability in decision-making can be seen in the fact that there are only four basic scenarios or routes to be taken. The differences below are based on the circumstances and resources available at that time, as well as any temporal constraints which may exist.

1. Authoritarian Route: This is where you look at a problem and make a decision without any input from others (classic one-way communication). In situations where time is of the essence and everyone is looking to you for an answer, you should use this route.

2. Informative Route: Here, timing isn't an issue; you don't have a fast-approaching deadline. Because of that, you can look at the problem, find a solution, and then present your solution to your group. After presenting your solution, you will explain how you reached your solution logically. Then you ask for their comments and thoughts. Going down this route, you're not involving your group in the decision-making process, but you are trying to make them feel involved because you're informing them. You can also use this route if you've made a decision that is unpopular, because it gives you an opportunity to convince others that it's a good idea.

3. Inclusion Route: This is usually the most popular route among your direct reports. Here, you present the group with the problem that needs to be solved, you ask for suggestions and recommendations, everyone discusses the possible solutions, and then you make a

decision. When using this route, you must be prepared to facilitate and mediate two-way communication. Make sure that you set aside enough time to go over all alternative solutions and that you give everyone a chance to speak. With this route, you're not only trying to find the best solution but also breeding creativity among your direct reports.

4. Delegating Route: When you take this route, you pass the decision-making process to someone else. You would use this route (1) if you want to try to develop one of your direct reports by giving them more responsibility, (2) because you're too busy to deal with the issue, or (3) because the problem falls under someone else's responsibility and not yours. It's vital when you delegate that you make the goals, objectives, and boundaries abundantly clear. It's your job to define your intent for the goals and the decision limits. After you've made the goals and decision limits clear, then you allow them to develop and execute a plan. This should be done with minimal supervision from you. Knowing when—and when *not*—to delegate is a part of being an effective leader.

Throughout the course of your life and your career, there will be people or experiences that help to shape you and hone your leadership skills. Without a doubt, for me, the biggest influence was the Marine Corps, followed by my time at John Deere and my college experience at Purdue University. The Marine Corps gave me a rock-solid foundation for leadership, John Deere taught me what leadership looks like in the civilian world, and Purdue University helped me bridge the gap and helped with my transition. I would be remiss if I didn't mention that raising my young daughter is certainly giving me additional insight into the nuances of leadership.

The military is the absolute best training ground for leadership, and most of the great leaders we have had in this country have one thing in common—military experience. If anyone is looking to learn, understand, and develop their leadership skills, there is no better venue. I am blessed to have had the opportunity to serve my country, and while there is no such thing as a *former Marine*, I regret that I am no longer active. The reason I am no longer active is I decided to stand firm on my convictions and the principles instilled in me during my training and ended up with an Honorable Discharge from the Marine Corps, and not a retirement package, which was there for the taking. I ended up having to make one of the toughest decisions in my life, and, given the circumstances, I have no doubt I made the right and honorable decision.

Early one Friday morning, the Marine Corps Detachment aboard Fort Leonard Wood mustered for a Battalion-run. I was one of thousands of Marines who participated in that morning PT session. As a Sergeant, I assisted with calling cadence, properly motivated individuals who needed to run faster, and continued on my day by reporting to my shop and performing my duties. The next morning, I woke up with an extremely sharp and throbbing pain behind my left knee. I could barely walk—and absolutely couldn't walk up or down my stairs for the entire day. The medical professionals at Fort Leonard Wood conducted a wide array of tests over the course of two years and found nothing wrong with my knee. Still, to this day, no one can tell me why I have pain and what is causing it. Over the course of my medical tests, I received advice from other older Marines. Some of them would explain that "everyone develops physical pain" as they age in the Marine Corps . . . and that "if you can still pass the PT-test, then you *can* stay in the Corps." That did not sit well with me. I truly wanted to stay in the Corps—but not that way. Part of being a Marine means that you hold yourself to high physical standards, standards you uphold just as those under your charge uphold. An image came to mind of me staying in the Marine Corps and telling my fellow Marines to charge a hill, when I couldn't even do it myself. That thought made my skin crawl. I couldn't do it, as I didn't want to be in a position where I expected something from my Marines that I couldn't expect from myself.

It wasn't an easy decision. I'd enlisted at the age of 18, and the Marine Corps was all I knew. I loved—and still love—"The Corps." It will always be part of who I am, as, at that time, I was the Marine Corps, and the Marine Corps was me. However, I could not fathom the prospect of looking in the mirror and calling myself a leader when my ability to perform a large part of "being a Marine" was lacking. I never wanted to order someone to do something that I could not expect from myself. I informed my superiors of my decision, and they immediately tried to get me to change my mind. I was offered a number of different options to stay in the Corps, however, I could not and would not attempt to lead from behind a desk or spend the rest of my career there. Grudgingly, they accepted my resignation. I was no longer in active service and was making the transition to civilian life. To this day, I have no regrets about that decision. I did not make that decision to make a point; I made it based on my convictions. And sometimes, that is what you must do—make a tough decision based on your convictions, as holding onto something that compromises your values and performance will only later tarnish your memories. You will think less of yourself, and, with that, others will think less of you.

As a leader, you will face many challenges, but the biggest challenge you will face will be yourself, usually as a result of complacency, apathy, or sheer indolence. The reasons for this are often because we are too inwardly focused. After constantly working on something, we generally become more talented, more skilled, and much more adept at the task or position. We start to feel good about ourselves, even giving ourselves a pat on the back from time to time. However, as we have all seen, past performance is no guarantee of future success, and if you think you can rest on your laurels or get by on your reputation, you are in for a rude awakening. Consequently, you lose focus and stop doing the things that got you there in the first place—that is, continually evolving and developing—as leadership is dynamic, not static, and you have to continue to adapt and grow. This usually happens over a long period of time and is often difficult to notice until it's too late to avoid it.

There are two important aspects to preventing this. The first is to be aware of this prospect, which you now are, since you're reading this. The next is to do something about it and have a regimen and process in place for continual assessment and development. There are a number of things you can do to stave this off, and here are a few steps I have taken that have worked best for me.

The first is the importance of a mentor or coach. I subscribe to the theory that two heads are better than one, so get two, which is what I have done. One of the mentors should be inside your business or industry, and the other one should be outside of it. These mentors will give you valuable insight and perspective that you otherwise would not have considered. They will also encourage you—and, hopefully, give you constructive criticism, which is a necessary component to growth.

The next is to schedule time for self-reflection and self-appraisal. Dr. Nando Pelusi states, "Self-appraisal is a necessary activity for navigating life. A conscious assessment of our goals, our behavior, our relationships, and our performance in all domains ultimately enables self-improvement. It allows us to expand our options in life." I too subscribe to this theory and make it part of my routine. As part of this process, one thing to keep in mind is that leadership blunders are inevitable. Everyone makes them, and it does not mean you are a bad leader. What is important is to honestly assess your behavior and traits, and take corrective action. When mistakes are made, acknowledge them, and move on. Learn from them, and don't dwell on them and beat yourself up unnecessarily. The other thing I strive to do is to create an environment where your direct reports are completely comfortable with giving you honest feedback about your performance as a leader. This exchange of information is valuable as it allows you and your team to constructively discuss things and gain a better understanding of why something is done the way it is. Your direct reports will give you more buy-in, since they are part of the solution. Give these three things a try. They have worked well for me, and I am confident they will work for you as well.

Looking at the obstacles I had to overcome, I would characterize it in two words—*toxic leadership*. One thing I did, and we all tend to do, is to put too much value in the actions, words, and thoughts of the leaders above you. We want them to be role models for us and behave in a manner that is consistent with the values of the organization and the individuals. However, when your idealistic view of leadership collides with reality, it hits you like a cold bucket of water, and you realize that just because someone is in a position of leadership and responsibility does not necessarily mean they are an effective leader.

As an example, in one instance during my time in the Marine Corps, I reported directly to an individual that I would characterize as a toxic leader. This individual would continually insult, berate, and even make fun of other Marines—of lower rank, I might add. Many of the comments were beyond the pale and had nothing to do with performance or results, were not motivating, and were extremely derogatory and personal in nature. It became more about a like or dislike for a certain person, ethnic group, etc., and no one was spared, whether in the unit or outside of the unit, and, more often than not, in front of fellow Marines. This type of toxic behavior attacked the dignity of the men and women who served under him, with the effects spreading like a disease which eroded morale, trust, and performance. This was an epiphany for me, as, prior to this, and afterwards, every leader I encountered engendered respect and trust, and represented the highest values of the Corps.

For a while I was disillusioned, even depressed, and let it affect my performance as I was not the leader that my

Marines knew me to be. Eventually, through introspection and soul-searching, I snapped out of it. I harkened back to my early days as a Marine and those values and codes of conduct which were central to being a good Marine. I realized those values and conduct were there—they were all around me— and that I could not let one individual's toxic leadership color my judgment or performance. I turned my attitude around; I vowed not to let one person affect me and my fellow Marines in such a manner, and we all pulled together. Eventually, as with most things, this individual's behavior caught up with him, and he was relieved of his position.

For me, it was a valuable lesson and a learning experience. Firstly, I realized that I had let myself and my fellow Marines down by letting one person's behavior have such a deleterious impact on me and chastised myself for losing faith for a while. It also reinforced the fact that any organization or company, no matter how well run, can have toxic leaders like this and that you need to have faith in the organization and the system. It also showed me firsthand the severe impact a bad leader could have on a group. Then and there I vowed always to represent the highest values and code of conduct in anything I did, anyone I worked for, and for anyone who was on my team.

Leadership is a multi-faceted issue, and, while everyone has their own predominant style, the important thing is not to become so rigid that you adhere to one style and are not able to adapt and shift gears based on the circumstances. My leadership style is somewhere between autocratic and *laissez-faire*. The best description I have heard so far is "Hands off, nose in." By this, I mean I am generally hands-off and won't micromanage you. I will let you succeed or fail and rise and fall on your own (as long as the fall doesn't kill you). I'm generally "nose in," meaning that I'm always asking a lot of questions. In the Marine Corps, being cognizant of those day-to-day activities is what we called "Small Unit Leadership," for which I am well suited. I'm a curious person by nature, and this helps me in leadership because leaders need to know what's happening on their team. I also strive to strike a good balance between strategy and day-to-day activities, with neither one at the expense of the other. And through all of this, my most important priority, and yours as well, should be the team. Focus on your team, observe them, review their performance, and put them in a position to succeed. They are a direct reflection of you, and it has always been my philosophy that leaders are selfless—they are there to serve others and develop those around them.

While a leader cannot be effective without the ability to adapt or pivot, there is one style or trait that fits all, which is the need to be authentic. Your style of dressing, your style of showing love to those you care about deeply, and your style of leadership are yours and cannot be duplicated. As you study, understand, and practice the universal basics of leadership and communication, you must find your own style of leadership. We can all spot a fake—someone who is trying to fit their round peg into a square hole, and I have been guilty of doing that as well. It isn't authentic and will come across that way. We will all experience that as we travel on our leadership journey, but it's important not to stay there. Those experiences are learning lessons; they are our bridges. In the same way that we don't stop on a bridge when our destination is home, we must leave those artificial experiences behind and go home.

Be true to yourself, and don't try to be something you aren't. Authenticity is the home of leadership.

As you go through your leadership journey, you will see that it is a continuum—you develop, improve, and keep learning. Through all of this, maintain your resolve and commitment, especially in the face of failure. You will assuredly have your failures, as you cannot predict the future, and that's okay. If you think of any person whom you consider successful, you probably know all about their achievements, victories, and triumphs. You rarely hear about their struggles, but I promise you that they have failed early and often. When you're faced with adversity and failure, know that a smooth sea never made a skilled sailor. Remember always to set a good example for others to emulate, and inspire others to the highest standards possible. Be patient, understanding, just, and firm. Praise the deserving and encourage the wayward. Focus on improving everyone around you, and ensure that, when you leave an organization, it is better than when you arrived.

In summary, the fact that you are reading this book and my chapter shows that you are taking leadership seriously. Most people don't; they understand only when it's too late. You are different. You care about leadership; you're earnest and sincere in your desire to be the best leader possible. The world needs more people like you. After you put this book down, go out and practice leadership. I guarantee that you will look back at your experiences with fond memories and be thankful that you started now, and not later.

CHAPTER SIX

JOHN BALLARD

★ ★ ★ ★ ★

Be Prepared to Lead

A graduate of the United States Air Force Academy, John Ballard rose to the rank of Lieutenant Colonel while reinventing Air Force management consulting, leading studies in organizations worldwide, including a two-year study of more than 37,000 medical personnel at 149 Air Force hospitals. Selected for doctoral study, Ballard earned his Ph.D. from Purdue University in Social-Personality Psychology minoring in Industrial/ Organizational Psychology. At the Air Force Manpower and Personnel Center near San Antonio, Texas, he led the Research and Measurement Division, managing all Air Force testing programs (more than 500,000 tests given annually), directing the Air Force Survey Program (more than 150,000 personnel surveyed annually), and determining requirements for Air Force human resources research and development projects (allocating more than $20 million annually). He began his academic *career at the Air Force's graduate school, the Air Force Institute of Technology (AFIT) near Dayton, Ohio, where he was honored as the Outstanding Professor in the Engineering Management Program and later as AFIT's Outstanding Professor of the Year. Retiring from the Air Force, he continued his career as a consultant, professor, and management scholar. He completed his academic career at Mount St. Joseph University in Cincinnati as Emeritus Professor of Management, where, in 2016, he received the Distinguished Scholar Award. Dr. Ballard has received numerous professional honors from the Academy of Management. In an international competition in 2016, his book,* Decoding the Workplace: 50 Keys to Understanding People in Organizations, *was honored as best Career book. More about John can be found here: http://www.johnballardphd.com/ about-john.html. He can be followed on Twitter at @JohnBallardPhD*

★ ★ ★ ★ ★

I NEVER ASPIRED TO BE A LEADER, to be seen as a leader. This may seem odd given my life history. As a teenager in the Boy Scouts, I moved through leadership positions from patrol leader, to senior patrol leader, to junior assistant scoutmaster. I attended and graduated from the United States Air Force Academy, an institution devoted to producing leaders for the U.S. Air Force and our nation. I had a successful Air Force career, obtained a Ph.D., and rose to the rank of Lieutenant Colonel. In my next career as a university professor, I taught management and leadership and led faculty, business school, and university committees—but I never sought to be a department chair or business school dean.

Do you have to aspire to be a leader to be seen as a leader? I think not. As I wrote in *Decoding the Workplace*, "Whether someone is a leader ultimately is a perception, an attribution made by a follower or followers about another person." Seeing yourself as a leader does not make you a leader. Someone else seeing you as a leader does. And keep in mind—in any group, some may see you as a leader, but others may not. There have been times in my life, moments in my life, when others saw me as a leader. How do I know? They told me.

I have had many management positions—some would say leadership positions. But to manage is not necessarily to lead. Not all managers are leaders. Not all leaders are managers. Management and leadership are not the same. One can manage, get the job done, without inspiring others, without motivating them to go the extra mile, to go above and beyond just doing their jobs. In my opinion, real leaders inspire others.

A leader in one situation may not be a leader in another situation. Michael Jordan was a leader playing basketball for the Chicago Bulls. He elevated the game of his teammates. But he took a break from basketball to try professional baseball. Was he as great a leader on the baseball diamond as he was on the basketball court? Not really. Leadership depends on the situation.

OK, you may ask: If being seen as a leader is a perception and being seen as a leader depends on the situation, how can I ever develop as a leader? In my opinion, the key to developing as a leader is your own personal growth, and personal growth continues throughout life. The motto of the Boy Scouts and Girl Scouts gets it right: "Be prepared." Be prepared to lead.

What follows are reflections from my life with insights that I think helped prepare me to lead or lead more effectively. I do not offer these insights as advice per se, just rules-of-thumb that in retrospect made a difference for me. Perhaps one or more may make a difference for you.

PERSEVERE

Persevering is an attitude. Stick-to-it-iveness. Not giving up. Doing all that you can to overcome obstacles to achieve your goal. If you have it, great. If it's not in your DNA, you can put it there. It is a mindset.

I probably developed the mindset to persevere in my youth as a Boy Scout. I wanted to attain the rank of Eagle. In the history of the Boy Scouts of America, only 4% of Boy Scouts have earned the Eagle rank. I knew if I stuck to it, I could accomplish the requirements and with time and effort earn most of the required merit badges. But I knew two merit badges would prove difficult—Lifesaving and Personal Fitness.

One of the requirements for the Lifesaving merit badge was to recover a 10-pound weight from 12 feet of water. Diving was hard for me. Today's requirement is only 8 to 10 feet. That I could have handled. But 12 feet? That seemed impossible. I took a lifesaving course at the local pool. I could demonstrate all the other requirements to save someone, but the diving down was just hard for me. As I got deeper, I could feel the pressure and the need for air. Over and over, for several weeks, I practiced breathing and diving. In practice, I was never successful. On the day of the diving test I failed four times, but on the fifth dive, I grasped the weight and pushed off to the surface. I know for many this would be a simple task, but for me it was a monumental achievement. It simply had to be done, and I stuck to it. The 10-pound weight was not the only weight lifted that day.

With the Personal Fitness merit badge, it was much the same. The difficulty was the pull-up requirement (which no longer exists). I had to do seven pull-ups, all executed with good form. I was stout and did not have much upper-body strength. But just like diving, I practiced, practiced, and practiced some more. I remained one short of the number needed. The best I could do was six. I decided to test for the merit badge anyway. When it was time for the pull-ups, I just said a prayer, gave it all I had, and just barely did seven pull-ups.

CONFRONT YOUR FEARS

In the fourth grade, I decided I wanted to be an architect and attend the U.S. Military Academy at West Point. By the seventh grade, I wanted to be a pilot, and that year I learned there was a West Point for the Air Force, the USAF Academy near Colorado Springs, Colorado. Attending the Air Force Academy became my dream, my goal. I knew it was physically, mentally, and emotionally demanding, but I thought I could survive. Only one thing truly disturbed me. I saw a film of cadets jumping from a 10-meter platform into the swimming pool. It looked so high. I knew sometime as a cadet I would be required to jump from that 10-meter diving platform into the water below. The thought of having to make that jump frightened me. It was my biggest fear.

I was fortunate and received a Congressional appointment to the Air Force Academy. That first summer was basic training, grueling, difficult, and demanding beyond anything I could have imagined. We just tried to survive from hour to hour, to get through the day. The only free time was a few hours on Sunday afternoons.

I knew what I had to do. So on that first Sunday, I went to the Athletic Center, to the Natatorium with its Olympic-size pool, to my nemesis, the 10-meter platform. It looked so much higher than its 33 feet. Several upperclassmen (i.e., sophomores, juniors, seniors) were taking turns jumping from the top of the tower. I watched for probably half an hour and then approached one of them.

"Sir, what do I need to know to jump off the tower safely?"

"The main thing is to jump away from the platform, cross your legs, try to enter the water as upright as you can. You going to do it?"

"Yes, Sir."

Slowly I climbed the stairs, occasionally looking down at the water. With each step the fear in me grew. I arrived at the top scared, alone, the water far below. My heart pounded, my body weak, my breathing labored. I walked to the edge. I did not look down. I stepped off away from the platform and crossed my legs: 1.4 seconds later at 35 mph I hit the water just slightly off center. For two days my body was sore, but my mind was at peace. I had done it. I had conquered my biggest fear. I knew that, when the time came when I would be required to make that jump, I could do it. The fear of that tower was behind me.

Later at the Academy, I had to make that jump surrounded by my classmates. Some jumped with no problem; a few even enjoyed it. But some were clearly scared. I was not. I had dealt with my fear privately. My demeanor was that of a leader— calm, assured.

DEVELOP YOUR ABILITY TO SPEAK
IN FRONT OF OTHERS

For many, this may be one of their greatest fears. I once was asked to emcee a small event, forty or so people, at the last moment. The room was full of accomplished, successful professionals. Part of the event was to be a few remarks from the attendees. Before the event began, I circulated among the attendees to arrange the order of the remarks. To my surprise, more than half said, "Sorry, I can't speak in public."

I understood. As a child, I'd had the lead in a Christmas pageant at my church. I knew my lines but was so frightened that I threw up and could not do it. In junior high school, I dreaded a teacher calling on me to read out loud. I was a good reader—but not in public.

I read about public speaking, looking for ideas to help me. Eventually I found one that actually worked—a breathing exercise. For decades I have shared this technique with others. Take a deep breath. Hold it briefly. Slowly let it out. Do this a few times. Now take a deep breath, hold it, slowly let it out, but before taking another breath, try to linger at the end of the exhaling. After exhaling there is a spot, a moment, in your chest where you feel totally relaxed. Look for that spot, and stay there briefly before the next breath. It is brief at first, but you can grow it. Continue doing this, staying at the relaxation spot longer each time. With just a little practice, you can find that spot and go there before speaking in public. It is a way to relax your body and mind. While I am waiting to speak, I do this with my regular breathing and let the relaxation spot do its magic. When I stand at a podium in front of many people, I take a breath, feel the spot, and then start speaking.

I know this technique has helped many people. Today I can speak in front of hundreds with no problems and usually enjoy the experience.

When people know you have no problem speaking in public, it opens doors and opportunities. I once was on a consulting team studying commissary (grocery) operations at Air Force bases throughout Europe. The team was composed of people from different functional areas. We did not know each other. At the end of each visit, the team chief gave a presentation about our findings to the base commander and senior staff. During one visit in Spain, the team chief became ill and asked for a volunteer to do the presentation to the senior staff. I volunteered, and, after that, I was the team member who did our presentations. When we were tasked to present our overall findings to the U.S. Commissary Service headquartered in Texas, I was asked to give that presentation. The officials there asked that I brief several generals at the Pentagon, which I did. These were good experiences made possible by my ability to speak effectively in front of people I did not know.

Whatever it takes, tackle public speaking. I have several friends who swear by Toastmasters. Good public speakers are not necessarily leaders, but the best leaders usually are.

BE AN EXPERT

An Air Force colonel once told me, "Know your job better than anybody else, and you'll be an expert." I have found this to be true. You may not start off in a job as an expert, but, by applying yourself, you usually can become an expert, even *the* expert, at what you do. Usually this will mean going above and beyond just doing the job, to truly master the job.

As a young Air Force officer, I chose to be in a career field called Management Engineering. It was mostly work sampling in various functions of an Air Force base to determine manpower requirements to accomplish the mission—but it also included consulting studies. I went to a ten-week training course to learn how to do the job. We spent one hour on consulting. When I asked the instructor why we spent so little time on consulting, he replied, "Because we don't really do it much, and, frankly, we don't know how." I was pretty bummed out, because consulting is why I chose that field.

At my first Air Force job, I talked with my boss, a captain, about my situation. He replied that the instructor was right, but there was one consulting project that had been bottom priority for a while. A couple of NCOs had been working on it off and on for more than a year with nothing really to show for it. I could take charge of it if I wanted to. I did.

After talking with the two people involved, I knew we were nowhere close to producing a result for the General Officer who had requested the study. I immersed myself in the literature of consulting, reading books and materials from established consultants. I talked with consultants at a Big Five consulting firm, Booz Allen Hamilton. I taught myself what I did not learn from the formal training.

We focused on an area of interest to the General, the base sports program, and completed the study in a few months. The General implemented all but one of our 52 recommendations. A year later, the General called me to his office. On his conference table was a very large trophy for having the best sports program from the 12 bases in the Air Training Command. Participation had doubled in a year. He thanked

me, "You made that happen," and asked that I congratu-
late my team. With that one success, consulting opportunities flowed our way at that base, from across Air Training
Command, and then from across the entire Air Force. I was
asked to draft procedures on how to do consulting studies for use by management engineers throughout the Air
Force. I went above and beyond and was seen as an expert.
This beginning to my career resulted in others seeing me
as a leader.

USE INITIATIVE

A General Officer once told me that, in his career, he had seen
two types of leaders. The first were leaders who innovated, took
risks, created new ways of doing things, used initiative. The
second were leaders who took the reins from the first type of
leaders and ran organizations effectively and efficiently. So you
can lead without using initiative, but using initiative increases
the odds that others will see you as a leader.

Initiative involves doing more than just what you are
told to do or the way you were told to do it—that is, seeing
opportunities, identifying problems, finding solutions, and
acting on them. It usually involves some degree of risk.
Sometimes the results of your initiatives work; sometimes
they may not.

As the president of the Junior Officers Council at an air
base early in my career, I represented the 1000 or so junior
officers (Lieutenants, Captains) on an Officers Club Advisory
Board. We met monthly, and it took only a few meetings to
realize the "O-Club" was not doing well; it was losing money.
The more senior officers on the board wanted to see the club

in the black, but no ideas were forthcoming. I knew that many of the junior officers just saw the club as stodgy, the place for a meal every now and then, or a drink or two. The club simply had little appeal to them.

I set up a meeting with the club manager to talk about some ideas that might attract more people to the club. Bottom-line: He told me if I wanted to try something, just do it. He'd give me a small budget.

In the heart of the O-Club was a large ballroom that was rarely used. With suggestions from my peers, my wife and I visited clubs in the area and found two bands that we thought would complement each other. We booked the ballroom for a Saturday night with a band at each end taking turns performing. We used layout principles to position the bars. It just happened that, because so few people had been dining at the club, there was a surplus of steaks. We arranged a two-for-one steak deal for that evening. The Saturday was the day after St. Patrick's Day, so we called our event "St. Patrick's Day +1," with continuous live music, two-for-one steaks, and a merry time guaranteed for all.

The event was an enormous success. It was the biggest night in bar revenue the club had ever seen. More importantly, we had demonstrated to club management how to attract more people and make the club successful. After that the ballroom had live music on weekends, and the club went from red into black. People knew I was President of the Junior Officers Council, but it was not until the success of "St. Patrick's Day +1" that I was actually perceived to be a leader by senior members of the Officers Club Advisory Board and the junior officers of the base community.

REFLECT AND BE INTROSPECTIVE

Active learning is built on the premise that we can learn by being more aware of what happens around us and then reflecting on that information. Most of us are not very good at this. We are not reflective or introspective. I designed my book *Decoding the Workplace* to encourage introspection and active learning, helping readers understand what is happening around them in the workplace. There is much information about ourselves in interactions with others to which we never attend. If we did, we might adjust a behavior or two and see if that makes any difference.

Carla was great at her job but did not interact much with her office colleagues. She was often the last to know new information about what was happening in the organization. Every day she brown-bagged her lunch and ate alone at her desk. Others also brown-bagged but ate together in the conference room. After reading about informal networks in the workplace and their impact on work, Carla reflected on the brown bags. She knew that she tended to be introverted and liked the quiet lunch in her office, but she wondered if it might be better to join the others in the conference room. So she tried it, and, to her surprise, through interacting with others, she became more in the loop at the office. As a result, she became even better at her job.

I developed this habit of reflecting and being introspective in my youth and have continued it through my lifetime. Emerging from these moments have been insights which I bounced off close friends. I have not always been successful in being a better me, but taking the time to think about situations and actions increased my effectiveness. The best leaders have self-knowledge. Know yourself.

There is also a benefit to taking time to reflect and think about where you are going. As an adult, I have made goals, reviewing and revising them annually. This also holds true in leading teams and organizations. We have a tendency to be reactive, not proactive.

As a young officer, I realized I was spending my days reacting, not planning. I could not get ahead of the curve. One day when I came to work, I told my secretary I did not want to be disturbed, to hold all calls unless from they came from very high in my chain of command. I went into my office, closed the door, and spent the entire day in my office thinking about our mission and what my part of the organization was really about. That day I developed an idea of where I wanted us to go and how we might get there. At the next meeting with my teams, I shared my thoughts and got their thoughts and feedback. Working together, we focused on more effective, meaningful training. With better skill sets came more success at our primary mission. And with that came promotions and recognition for my teams. If you understand your priorities, you make time to reflect—on your work and your life.

THE SITUATIONAL NATURE OF LEADERSHIP

Few of us will be leaders in every situation. Most of us will have opportunities to lead at some point. Sometimes to lead we must step forward. Other times, it just happens, and we aren't even aware of it. In retrospect one of my most meaningful experiences as a leader was one in which I was not even aware I was being seen as leading.

In 1991 my friend Richard Bilodeau and I traveled to the Big Island of Hawaii to hike up Mauna Loa to see a total eclipse of the sun. [The first part of the story is told at the website redhillsolareclipse.com and completed in the Kindle short story *Miracle at Red Hill: A Total Solar Eclipse Adventure.*] To make our hike, we needed climbing passes from the National Park Service. We arrived at the Kilauea Visitor Center on a Friday to obtain the passes. We were told passes would be issued Monday. There was no specific time. There was no specific number of passes per person. We were concerned that just a few people or agencies would get the 100 passes to be available or that there would be a mob jostling to get passes. Surely we were not the only ones who realized seeing a total solar eclipse high on a volcano would be an experience of a lifetime. In short, there was an absence of planning.

We arrived at the Visitor Center early on Saturday morning. Working with the Chief Park Ranger, we shared our concerns. He understood them and worked with us to resolve the issues. The Park Service decided on a limit of four permits for a group and an exact time for the issuing of climbing permits to begin, 7:45 a.m. on Monday. The Chief put this in writing and posted it for everyone to see.

Satisfied with the policy, we saw only one issue remaining: How to avoid chaos Monday morning. My solution: Treat it like a rock concert and form a first-come, first-in admission line. After all, a total solar eclipse is one of the greatest shows on Earth. For rock concerts, the bigger the event, the earlier the line starts forming. I explained the idea of a line to the Chief. He liked it and gave permission for the line to form on Sunday. He had rangers show us where the line could start and where the line should be located as it lengthened. The line formed at midnight—12:00 a.m. Sunday morning—grew through the night. By Sunday mid-morning, there were more than 50 in line; Monday morning, nearly 100. In groups of four, we got our permits and were taken in a Park Service van to the trailhead. On Tuesday I found the spot from where I wanted to see the eclipse. Wednesday morning I was there. Two rangers joined me. The shadow of the moon descended, and the majesty of a total solar eclipse unfolded over the volcanic wilderness. Later, in a mist, Richard and I hiked down. I had an issue with a foot that slowed my pace, so we arrived after the time for the last Park Service van back to the Visitor Center. To our surprise, a Park Service van appeared.

"We heard you were coming down. Heard you might be arriving late. Thought we ought to check."

Richard and I were very grateful. We would either have had to continue our hike for miles or pitch our tent for the night.

On the way back, the ranger talked with us.

"Just want you to know we really appreciated how you took charge and organized the people going up the mountain. We had another group who wanted passes for their RVs a few weeks ago, and it was not pleasant. We had figured last Monday would be the same, but it was smooth and easy, thanks to you."

After we were dropped off, Richard and I headed to our cabin and then to dinner.

"John, you know you were the leader up there."

Surprised, I asked, "What do you mean?"

"You heard the ranger. You organized everybody, set up the system, and people knew it. Why do you think people sought you out? Why do you think the rangers on the volcano wanted to be with you during the eclipse? I've seen you lead before, but this was the most impressive."

Reflecting on those days in Hawaii, I came to agree with Richard. You may never know when your leadership will emerge. You may not even be aware you are leading. But there are other times you may be called on to lead or choose to lead. Be prepared.

CHAPTER SEVEN

MICHAEL H. MILLER

★ ★ ★ ★ ★

VADM (retired) Michael Harold "Mike" Miller was born and raised in Minot, North Dakota. He was awarded a Bachelor of Science degree from the United States Naval Academy and earned his "Wings of Gold" at Pensacola, Florida. Subsequent flying tours were primarily out of Naval Air Station Cecil Field, Florida, flying the S-3A/B Viking on carrier deployments around the world, including multiple combat operations against Libya, the Achille Lauro *terrorist incident, and squadron command in the Persian Gulf during Desert Shield/Desert Storm. During his distinguished career, he was in command of the 3rd Fleet Flagship,* USS Coronado *(AGF11) and later the* USS John F. Kennedy *(CV67), where he had an extended deployment to the Persian Gulf. After command of the* Kennedy, *Miller became the first active-duty officer to direct the White House Military Office as well as commissioned as a Deputy Assistant to the President. He then assumed command of Carrier Strike Group 7 and led the* USS Ronald Reagan *Strike Group on its maiden deployment to the Persian Gulf and the Western Pacific. After a tour as the deputy chief of staff for Global Force Management & Joint Operations, he reported to Capitol Hill as the Chief of Legislative Affairs, the Navy's point man for all Naval programs and policy. Following this, he returned to his roots, becoming the 61st Superintendent of the U.S. Naval Academy. He retired from the Navy after this tour, earning the distinction of being one of the most highly decorated graduates in the history of the Naval Academy. Following his retirement from active service, Miller has continued to pursue his passion for education, cybersecurity, and aviation logistics through various boards and public forums.*

★ ★ ★ ★ ★

LEADERSHIP IS ONE OF THOSE TOPICS that always comes to the fore in any organization, since the tone and strategy for success inevitably evolve from the company's leadership philosophy. While the focus and importance of leadership is relevant to just about anything that gets accomplished, the velocity of the change taking place in today's workspace presents a host of challenges and questions that many modern leaders have not faced previously. With flattened hierarchical structures, continual work turnover, and ever-evolving company goals, there is probably no more difficult question than "What is leadership?" While definitions and concepts are plentiful, if you stacked every book ever written on leadership, you would undoubtedly surpass the height of the Empire State Building and still not be able to answer the question in its totality. From my perspective, "leadership" is the ability to motivate others to unite for a common cause or a set of goals, built on a foundation of teamwork, trust, and camaraderie, which leads to personal growth that encourages members of the team to exceed their goals and aspirations.

The best leaders I have witnessed always took a proactive approach to goal setting and achievement, as opposed to "reactive" leadership, which is more commonly known as "crisis management." For me, it is important to make a distinction between "leadership" and "management." One focuses on individual/team growth and achievement, while the other favors extensive measures of productivity. Management is typically easier to measure, as it is more task oriented; the desired outcome can be metricized and then checked to see if the correct numbers are produced. Unfortunately, it is all too common for those in management positions to fall into "If the minimum wasn't good enough, it wouldn't be the minimum" trap. In other words, if management isn't really focused, the tendency will be to set a low bar. Everyone feels like they are getting the job done, but no one is reaching their full potential. I have spent a great deal of time with some remarkable managers who always knew how to make the bottom line and get that number—but the only reason their employees followed them was out of pure curiosity.

"Leadership," on the other hand, is far more nuanced. It's much more than numbers and, therefore, much more difficult to measure, because it's really about the way the members of the team feel about themselves and their contribution to the overall effort. If applied properly, leadership yields many aspects of personal growth that can and should exceed even the expectations of the individual members of the team. Moreover, leadership often involves decisions that can be life-altering or even life-threatening, and these goals and aspirations cannot be easily translated into dollars and cents. For all the lectures I've attended or books that I have read on leadership, I have never found that "silver bullet" or "one-size-fits-all" approach. It seemed like every time I'd think I was getting things just right, something unforeseen and, more often than not, beyond my control, would raise its ugly head, which necessitated a course correction and/or rebuilding the team. In hindsight, it wasn't necessarily a bad thing for me or my organization. These constant fluctuations kept me on my toes and resulted in personal and professional growth. Just as importantly, as I worked with the team members on making the necessary changes and ironing the kinks out, it also resulted in team members learning and growing. In this respect, as a matter of perspective, I always looked at challenges I faced as a leader as opportunities for change and growth, as opposed to simple obstacles.

One of the age-old questions is "Are leaders born or made?" My view is that great leaders are forged by the experiences of their lifetimes. There are a multitude of reasons for individuals to be put in charge of others—family ties, educational background, diversity, age, physical fitness, and personal charisma, to name but a few, but being "put in charge" doesn't mean that individual is therefore a leader by some sort of divine right. The most effective leaders I have witnessed are invariably graduates of "the School of Hard Knocks." Their willingness to extend themselves into unfamiliar circumstances means that they have chosen the road less traveled and, with that, they have faced a much greater risk of failure. Their ability to make decisions, make mistakes, and learn from each is their calling card. But without this proclivity and this drive to expand their horizons, aspiring leaders will never find the space necessary to build their character or develop the skills and confidence to act despite a great deal of uncertainty.

There are numerous examples of great leaders who have come from a long line of distinguished family heroes. Their lineage would seem to imply that they were, in fact, "to the manner born." On the other hand, what I have witnessed is that these "lineage leaders" were taught early in life of their family's expectations and were held to very high standards. Their irrepressible drive to succeed, and even exceed, the achievements of their ancestors wasn't handed down genetically but, rather, imbued through the extra efforts of their families, mentors, and teachers.

Not everyone is cut out to be a leader, and there are many obstacles to overcome. These are not obvious at first, but, over time, they become apparent, and, in particular, one became apparent for me. In the summer of 1970, I landed at National Airport in Washington, DC, having been accepted into the U.S. Naval Academy. I arrived with the same hopes and aspirations that most college freshmen hold, except that I was going to be attending a military institution. I was a country kid, having grown up in North Dakota, but my intention was to serve in the Navy, preferably as a carrier aviator. There were two small challenges associated with this plan: first, I had never seen the ocean (or the Academy, for that matter), and, secondly, I had never been in an airplane. So, not surprisingly, my initial exposure to a military lifestyle came as quite a shock.

The course of education at Annapolis is rigorous, especially in the first year as a "plebe," or freshman. The school's intent was to screen out those who weren't "tough enough" or lacked the tenacity to face academic, physical, and emotional stress simultaneously. To say that I was unprepared for this world is an understatement of the highest order. I had been raised in a family relatively devoid of controversy and strife. We didn't argue or yell at each other, and while I could get out of hand as much as any other teenager, my Mom and Dad were relatively mild in their discipline and fairly quick to forgive my many shortcomings. Most notably, I was (and remain) an introvert, living in a world that tends to be run by extroverts. Military service, on the other hand, requires all of its leaders to step up when the occasion calls for their guidance. There is little time for self-reflection, and, in certain circumstances, self-doubt, as decisions must be made in a matter of split seconds. The Naval Academy was instrumental in teaching me when to speak up, but it was neither an easy nor pretty process. The Academy's core values of "Honor, Courage, and Commitment" were the fundamental building blocks upon which I learned to accept my responsibilities, understand my accountability, and how to motivate others to pursue those same goals.

What are the characteristics of an effective leader? Every philosopher since Socrates—and perhaps even earlier—has attempted to synthesize the qualities of great Leaders. Based on my years of leadership and command, I have boiled my list down to seven critical "keystones" that seem to be at the core of every great leader I have met. I have also taken the liberty of relaying some "sea stories" in an attempt to exemplify these traits.

1. Humility. On the evening of January 20th, 2001, President George W. Bush entered the Oval Office with his father, our 41st President, George H.W. Bush. For the son of the former President, it must have been a surreal moment, having watched his father wrestle with a global uncertainty that was unimaginable just a few years before. For all the turmoil of a contested election, establishing a new administration, and immediately facing threats across the globe, our 43rd President set about his work mindful of those who had preceded him, humbled by their efforts, and grateful for the shoulders upon which he stood. The change in the White House was immediate and palpable. From the dress code to the discipline within the senior staff, the civility and humility that the President demonstrated in those first few days set an example and a standard for all to emulate.

2. Courage. Most people are familiar with the story of Apollo 13 and the extraordinary heroism of three great Americans who, when faced with the incredibly dangerous and challenging circumstances of an explosion in space, successfully returned their crippled spacecraft to earth. While the heroics of the crews, both in the capsules and on the ground, are the stuff of legend, I can't help but reflect on a conversation I had with Captain Jim Lovell, who was the mission commander on this ill-fated attempt at a lunar landing. As has been reported in numerous forums, Captain Lovell relayed to me the basics of their successful return, a rough recollection of which went like this: "I knew where

we needed to go (Earth), and I had a rough idea of what that trajectory would look like if the computer systems were calculating it. So, I put a grease mark on the observation window aligned with where I thought we would need to re-enter and tried to keep the ship pointed consistently at that spot." He said this with such plain-spoken honesty and such humility that I was speechless. Sometimes, leadership is just about having the courage to "make the grease mark" and stick to it.

3. Respect. Regardless of the size of the organization or how steep the pyramid required to rise to a leadership position, the best leaders I've witnessed found a way to encourage growth without rancor. I'll admit there are always going to be some employees who just can't (or won't) fit in, but if the leadership is willing to invest time and energy into helping a team member become more of a positive force in the organization, more often than not, that team member can be turned around. You also have to be aware and accept that there will be times when a team member cannot be turned around—and can't be "saved"—while at the same time sifting through the barrage of commitments in an attempt to improve. In one of my commands, I had a team member who simply couldn't fit in . . . and it wasn't due to a lack of effort on our part. This individual was openly critical of our organization, and I was initially taken aback by the vitriol that this person came to represent. And yet, looking back on it, this one individual helped crystallize our goal setting and bring into focus all that was right with our organization. Don't get me wrong—this

employee possessed the "courage of his convictions," but, in dealing with this challenge to our leadership team, we came to a much stronger understanding of who we were and why other opinions needed to be heard. Most importantly, we learned to respect the naysayers in our organization, for they, too, had a story to tell.

4. Trust. Storms out at sea can defy description. Many folks have seen the movie *The Perfect Storm*, and that account provides insight into the extraordinary risks of life at sea. In December of 1997, we had been on a forward deployment onboard the aircraft carrier *USS Saratoga* for roughly six months. As Yuletide slowly approached, we were informed that we wouldn't be home for Christmas. Doesn't sound like much, I'm sure, but being away for half a year and being so close to attending family gatherings that we had all looked forward to, well, we junior aviators just couldn't understand it. The Captain of the ship, one "CB" Hunter, was sympathetic to the malaise that had slowly settled over his ship and wanted to do something about it. The challenge was a huge storm in the Atlantic that stood directly between us and our home port in Jacksonville, Florida. We had pretty much accepted our fate and were in the process of writing letters informing our loved ones that, despite our promises, we wouldn't be home for Christmas when the Captain came on the ship's intercom system. "CB" indicated that the navigation team had devised a strategy to get us home on time but only if we could "batten down the hatches" and

make the ship and aircraft secured for heavy weather. Needless to say, every sailor on that ship worked tirelessly to ensure the *Saratoga* could face the impending storm. Now, aircraft carriers are huge ships, and the *Saratoga* was no exception, but the violence associated with a large mid-Atlantic storm is nothing to be trifled with. Yet the Captain had determined that, with the trust and support of his crew, the ship could safely navigate through the jaws of this monster. Captain Hunter put his trust in us and every shipwright who had ever worked or welded on the *Saratoga*, and as a consequence, after enduring the highest seas I had ever witnessed to that point, we arrived home safely on December 23rd. I came to realize, many years later, the tremendous risk the Captain had taken on our behalf, and I can't think of him without an upwelling of gratitude for his humility, courage, and trust that led to one of the best surprise Christmas presents my mother ever experienced. "CB" had earned our trust, and his calm, thoughtful decision-making inspired me and many of my contemporaries to pursue a lifetime of service to others.

5. Teamwork. Regrettably, that Atlantic storm was not to be the last that we would experience during my time in the Navy. On September 15, 1999, a Category 4 hurricane which was heading up the east coast of the U.S. overran an oceangoing tug, the *Gulf Majesty*. We were embarked on another aircraft carrier, this time, the USS *John F. Kennedy*, and had sortied early out of our homeport in Jacksonville to successfully

outrun the storm to the west of us. Hurricane Floyd was enormous, one of the largest Atlantic storms ever recorded, and, as it caught up with the *Gulf Majesty*, her unrelenting winds gradually pulled the tug under, still attached to the barge the *Gulf Majesty* was towing. As we continued east to avoid the storm, we received a call from the Coast Guard indicating that they had lost contact with the tug shortly after receiving a "Mayday" call from the vessel. In quick succession, an emergency position indicating radio beacon ("EPIR" for short) went off in the general vicinity of where the *Gulf Majesty* had last reported her position. No further radio responses were received, the Coast Guard was on the wrong side of the storm, and we were in the only position that had a chance of helping the crew to survive. While the *JFK* had embarked our helicopter squadron, the remainder of the Airwing had flown to much-safer Naval Air Stations further from the reach of this Atlantic juggernaut. The decision then became quite simple: Do we risk the ship and crew by heading into these fifty-foot seas and one hundred and fifty-five mile-per-hour winds in an attempt to save a small crew of eight, or do we stay further to the east, safely let the storm pass us by, hoping that these seamen could survive for several days as the storm proceeded to the north? Thanks to some excellent meteorological analysis on the *JFK*, a supportive staff, and some superbly trained helicopter crews, the decision was made to proceed into the teeth of Floyd, and to stay there as long as required to rescue this stranded crew. As an epilogue to the story, the helicopter crews were able to first find three of the seamen from the *Gulf Majesty* clinging to a broomstick, with an EPIR attached to one of their vests, riding what they described as a "fifty foot roller coaster that never seemed to end." About two hours later, our helicopter crews located the tug's orange inflatable lifeboat with the remaining five crew members inside—battered and bruised, but thankful to be alive. While one would hope that no leader is ever forced to make life-and-death decisions in moments of such extreme stress, you must be prepared, and my experience tells me that, in those extreme instances, the team that is well prepared for every eventuality will ultimately triumph.

6. Optimism. I believe that a healthy, optimistic view of every challenge has a multiplying effect on everyone else's confidence in their own abilities. In one unusual circumstance, we were faced with the inability to meet payroll, a rare occurrence in and of itself, given that we were a government entity. Because it was an unprecedented event, there was, understandably, a great deal of angst associated with not receiving a paycheck. This subsequently led to a great deal of speculation about how long this would last, how we would pay our bills, our mortgages, support our kids in school, keep our leased cars, keep the lights on, etc. Although our organization was composed of extremely intelligent and thoughtful individuals, I found that many could fall into the pit of despair with just the slightest push or circumstance. Rather than take the "low road" and

assume that "all is lost," our leadership team instead chose to build a hierarchy-of-needs profile that enabled us to see who was actually on the brink. We then developed a plan to provide the loans or financing to ensure that no one was left stranded, out of money, and out of ideas. Fortunately, the government shutdown didn't last long, and, in the end, everyone was fully reimbursed, even for days that they didn't or couldn't work. Yet, for me, it was a lesson in facing each challenge as an opportunity and seeking the best way to reassure every employee that they would be taken care of. The end result would not have been any different, but the toll on our employees who would endure sleepless nights and stressful days was successfully averted—with just a healthy dose of optimism.

7. Honesty/Integrity. Finally, and most importantly, every great leader must possess the character that enables them to earn the trust, build the team, demonstrate the courage, optimism, and humility that will inspire others to respect their guidance, and rise to meet every challenge. I have purposefully listed this last, for it is truly the foundation upon which every leader must stand. Not one of the attributes that precede this are worth a hill of beans if the leader can't be counted upon to demonstrate that he/she knows the "hard right" from the "easy wrong." In this age of instant communications, social media, and blogs that embrace virtually every point of view, it is essential that the leader repeatedly shows the way to "True North" and keeps the organization's moral compass properly

aligned. Absent that consistent dedication to honesty and integrity, no unit, company, or organization can survive in the long run.

Looking back, at each level of my professional development, the importance of mentors was of incalculable value, and I was blessed to have many who were willing to share their thoughts and wisdom. For most who will read this epistle, the tragedy of the 9/11 attacks on the World Trade Center and the Pentagon will be but a paragraph or perhaps a chapter in a history book. But as one of the few who were able to view the devastation firsthand in both New York City and Washington, DC, on that dark day, I must confess to having experienced a certain amount of despair. So much fear, so many unanswered questions. It was written on the faces of everyone I saw late on September 11, 2001. Everyone, except the President of the United States. His strength became our strength; his resolve, our resolve; his decisiveness a beacon for a nation desperate for a light to guide our footsteps into an uncertain new reality. I can still recall him setting his jaw—and we all knew then that the days of Bin Laden were numbered. Our 43rd President was and continues to be a source of inspiration for me, and I am thankful for the lessons I learned during my time with him.

In a leadership position, you are always learning. And, as I mentioned earlier, I was more of an introvert when I started out and was content to sit back and observe as opposed to being out front. I developed a knack for listening and focusing on the issues at hand. However, with each increase in responsibility came a greater desire to "fix things," and, as I gained more experience, it became more and more difficult to accept less than the best from myself and my teammates. As a result, there were certain tactics that I employed that were central to my effectiveness that may be worth noting.

I observed that, in many instances, one of the obstacles to improvement was simply a matter of communication, and, in this respect, simply listening was not effective, as there was not a free exchange of ideas. Consequently, when I took on my first divisional leadership role, I took it one step further and would simply ask, "If you had the power, what would you change in our outfit, and how would you do it?" By doing this, it changed into a Q & A or discussion as opposed to just "a bitch session." These exchanges generated a lot of feedback and questions, and they became part of the solution. Afterwards, I would publish a list of our top priorities, which later became known as simply "The Top Ten," although some of my staff referred to them as "The Ten Commandments." This process reinforced our key issues and operating parameters and helped put everyone on the same page. It also proved its value later, when, quite literally in the heat of battle, folks had to make important decisions in my absence.

Another issue is the decision-making process. The need for objectivity and accuracy is foremost if a leader is to make the right decision. When I say "objectivity," I mean that a leader needs to be as impartial as possible and understand that each situation, in and of itself, is unique. I have become convinced that we are not the "beneficiaries of our experiences" but rather the "victims of our experiences." In so many ways, our biases, even bigotry, are founded on small experiences, ingrained in our psyche, and subsequently applied to a wide variety of situations that may on the surface appear similar but on so many occasions have little relevance to what our "experiences" are telling us. This "group-think" or "confirmation bias" can have far-reaching implications if assumptions are not tested or questioned, critical facts not considered or ignored, and the consequences of the decision not fully understood. My *modus operandi*, when time permitted, was to examine the issue from all angles and secure as much input as possible. The bigger the issue, usually the more time it will take to crystallize a well-thought-out approach that involves the stakeholders in the analysis and development of the plan. I instilled in my team a sense of accountability and initiative, as well as a perspective of "we all own this challenge" with any issue or problem raised having an accompanying recommendation or solution. And even after all of that, a leader needs to understand that things do not always go as planned and that mistakes will be made. A good leader will accept accountability, take the time to analyze the mistakes, and then get on with business, ensuring the same mistakes are not repeated in future instances.

A leader also needs to understand that "one size never fits all" because the equation involves more than just the leader—it involves every member of the team. As an example, every team or workforce has a mixture of extroverts and introverts, and these groups respond to leadership in different ways. When attempting to adopt new ideas and strategies, you need to give them—and the organization—time to assimilate and absorb significant changes. Introverts will not naturally wish to stand up in a public forum and question the wisdom of their leaders; they need to have their internal debate on what these changes might mean. You need to afford them the opportunity to replay in their head what you have said and then have a dialogue to ensure you get their input and listen to their response. By the same token, you will always have some extroverts who are quite expressive or opinionated; you have to ensure you siphon off the emotion and home in on their facts. You also need to be cognizant of team-busting behavior and wary of someone or a group trying to dominate or intimidate someone, so that everyone has a chance to respond.

I have often been asked, "What is the biggest challenge a leader faces?" Here, I will use a metaphor. I once served on a ship that went into a dry dock, which is to say, completely out of the water and resting on its keel. I was amazed at the amount of sea-growth that had developed over the years on the hull of the ship, under the water, unobserved by any of us who worked on and in the ship. But those barnacles were slowing us down, literally, as they interfered with the smooth flow of water across the ship's hull. Similarly, I think many organizations develop these same "barnacles" in their business practices and processes. Every time I heard the "because we've always done it that way" explanation to a question, I was off on another adventure in discovering how our organization functioned and how we could improve our production/success rate (our "speed" if you will) while increasing our understanding of exactly what we were doing. Most importantly, sometimes "scraping the barnacles" can reveal unethical or questionable behavior that has become inculcated into the organization's culture. Without question, these processes, once discovered, must become the leader's first priority. No organization can succeed for long once "True North" is lost and it begins to ignore the company's moral compass. These behaviors frequently start small but, like barnacles, grow over time. In some cases, I relied on outside auditors to help me get to ground truth, and, in others, the remedies were so obvious that the changes could be made quickly. The challenge then became how to clearly articulate where we had gone astray and what we were going to do to get ourselves back on the right path.

From "scraping barnacles" to developing a company culture that is both an object of pride and worthy of emulation, a leader is pulled in so many different directions. In this respect, I hope this has given some direction to those of you who have taken the time to read this. I would like to close by offering one of my favorite quotes, from Heraclitus (B. 535 B.C.) "No man ever steps in the same river twice, for it is not the same river, and he is not the same man." I always tried to remember that wisdom in dealing with everything from the mundane to the monumental. Leadership is a journey, with many rivers to cross, and, while some might look identical, none will ever be.

CHAPTER EIGHT

THOMASINA SKIPPER

★ ★ ★ ★ ★

*Thomasina Etheridge Skipper was born in Cleveland,
Ohio. She earned her bachelor's degree from Syracuse
University with a major in Political Science and a minor
in Economics; she later earned an MBA form Kennesaw
State University, with honors. Thomasina began her career
with Fireman's Fund Insurance Company in Cleveland,
Ohio, as a Personal Lines Underwriter and, over her
career, took on positions of increasing responsibility. She
was the General Manager of Citizen Insurance Agency,
an independent insurance agency, an Agency Manager
for State Farm Insurance Company, and an Agency Field
executive for State Farm Insurance agency. With a strong
interest in leadership, she has attained numerous certi-
fications, awards, and is a sought-after speaker, consultant, and coach. She is a Charter Financial Consultant,
ChFC, a Charter Life Underwriter, CLU, and a Chartered
Leadership Fellow, CLF. She is licensed as a Certified
Professional Business Coach by the Professional Business
Coach Alliance (PBCA). Thomasina was Awarded 2021*

Business Coach of the Year in the United States from the Professional Business Coach Alliance (PBCA). She has been the keynote speaker at numerous conferences and meetings such as GAMA, International LAMP conference, Insignia Life, Farm Bureau Insurance Company, and Woodmen of the World Insurance Company. She is a member of the GAMA speaker's bureau and a visiting lecturer for the American College. She is President/Owner of Thomasina Skipper, Business Growth Specialist Coaching & Consulting Firm, and a founding principal of Diversified Professional Coaches, LLC. Thomasina is also a workshop facilitator and presenter on Business Management, Diversity & Inclusion, and People Development; she has co-authored the book Women Matter: The Why and How of Gender Diversity in Financial Services, *with Daralee Barbara and Linda Witham.*

★ ★ ★ ★ ★

LEADERSHIP IS SOMETHING that has always intrigued me. My MBA had a concentration in leadership, I have received a designation from the American College as a Chartered Leadership Fellow, and my personal library has more books on leadership than on any other topic. I have embraced the topic and would characterize myself as having a mild obsession around the subject of leadership. In putting this chapter together, it dawned on me that one reason for my obsession is that I have experienced very few opportunities of truly being led. I'm not sure if it is due to working in a white-male-dominated environment of insurance and financial services as a black female, or if I have somehow idealized the topic of leadership. However, I know that leadership matters. While I have rarely been the beneficiary of great leadership, where and when I had the opportunity to experience it firsthand, I observed, learned, and sought to emulate those traits that exemplified the best practices of leadership as I honed my craft.

Leadership and the ability to lead others—is it a skill or a talent? Can you learn to lead, or do you have to be born with the natural ability of leadership? I am sure you are familiar with the phrase "natural-born leader," which assumes that some people are simply born to lead, and some are not. Perhaps we would call these people "un-natural-born" leaders! I've read many books and articles on the subject, and the answers are all over the place. I also recall taking a leadership course in which leadership was defined as an element of "follow-ship." The premise was that, before you can be a great leader, you must be a great follower. These are just a few examples to make the point that the concept of leadership can be concrete or abstract—depending on who you're talking to and the situation you find yourself in. And there is no absence of articles out there to buttress any position you wish to take.

For this chapter, I proceed under the premise that leadership talents are within each of us, which I truly believe is the case, as we all have the potential to lead in some capacity or manner. Some of us have an overabundance of that talent, with it near the surface of our character and personality. Others may have less of that potential, with it being deeper and requiring more focus to draw on that talent. Raw talent that is not developed into a skill is just that—raw talent with potential. However, for this potential to be realized, this talent must be nurtured and that skill developed. Here, I am firmly on the side of Malcolm

Gladwell in the nature versus nurture argument; he makes a compelling case in his book *Outliers* that nurture wins the day. The same holds true when it comes to someone who wants to develop and improve their leadership skills.

Speaking of developing, in retrospect, it was the sum of my experience which enabled me to turn my potential into a skillset. The groundwork was there, but so were the warning signs! I was the youngest of four daughters in a family in which accountability and education were emphasized. I was not an easy child to raise, as I was always pushing the envelope, questioning things, and standing my ground, especially with three older sisters. I was also very curious, had a craving to learn, and was a voracious reader. When I wasn't in school or training for one of my sports activities, you would find me at the library, which, to my delight, was a treasure trove of information. I managed to excel in school and became the first person in my family to attend college via an academic scholarship to Syracuse University. It was also there that I realized I was a minority; back then, if you came from East Cleveland, you pretty much stayed there, so my scope was not very broad.

I also became acutely aware of the fact that, despite my academic record, I was woefully unprepared for the academic rigors. Many of the topics were foreign to me, and I had not had the benefit of going to prep school, which was the case with many of the students. Nonetheless, I reverted to form and spent countless hours at the library, in this case studying, instead of devouring as many books as I could. I put the time in and vowed to make my family proud, and then—they weren't. My senior year at Syracuse, I found out I was going to be a mother, and to the chagrin of the father and my family, I decided he would not be a good life partner for me. I decided to become a single parent with a child. I make this distinction because I, in no way, viewed the child as "illegitimate," which was the prevailing sentiment. That spawned a series of circumstances and hardships such that I could not finish the last semester at Syracuse due to financial constraints. "We" moved back to Cleveland, and, to survive, I had to go on welfare for a brief period. It was humbling, but I have always been thankful for this bridge, as it enabled me to finish college at Cleveland State University and then land a job at Fireman's Fund. As a single parent, and one of two black females in the entire company, I proudly entered the workforce as an underwriting trainee, no longer having to depend on welfare, and was able to raise my daughter. After five years at Fireman's Fund, I had the opportunity to further my career and took other positions of greater responsibility in the insurance industry. After several years of moving up the ranks, I was promoted to an Agency Manager and moved to Atlanta, Georgia, as only the third African-American woman in the company. I oversaw a team of twenty agents, of whom only two were African American—one man and one woman.

For those not familiar with the insurance industry, it has a reputation for hiring people, burning them out, and then flushing them out of the industry. The Life and Health part of the industry has a 13% retention after four years. Multiline Insurance Agencies are only slightly better, with a retention rate of less than 50% after two years. Suffice it to say the insurance industry has a terrible reputation—that is well earned—for churning people. However, the industry has also some of the best and brightest leaders I have met.

With this as a backdrop, I vowed that would not be the case on my watch. I now viewed my position differently and saw myself as not so much "in the insurance business" as in the "talent-management business." My emphasis, rightly so, had shifted, and my primary focus was to seek out the most talented people, invest in their development, and then get out of their way and let them flourish! This approach coincided with my belief that a great leader should pour into their people and focus on helping them to become their best selves, which is what I did. I looked at each person, assessing their skill set, including strengths and weaknesses, and developed a plan to build their skills and enhance their performance. It was a real win-win, as the company benefited due to my group leading the country in sales volume while having the highest retention rate in the agency. The problem for me had reversed itself: retention rates were no longer an issue, and I had a consistent flow of candidates eager to join up with me.

When I am asked what the biggest challenges are that I have faced in a leadership position, my answer is always the same—the people I report to and the people who report to me and are entrusted to my care. As I alluded to earlier, the number of people I reported to that I considered good leaders paled in comparison to the number that I felt were subpar. This was due to several things. In many instances, people were promoted simply because they had performed well in one function but were then placed into a leadership position, in which they had little to no leadership experience or acumen. This was a disservice to the individual who was promoted, since he or she was being set up for failure. Similarly, it was not fair to the people under that leader since they were not properly developed or nurtured. In some instances, people were placed in those positions simply because they were easy to work with and had a "go along to get along" approach. They followed the party line, went along with everything, never challenged anything, and never rocked the boat.

If you read the last sentence above again, you have just read the exact opposite of who I am and how I operate. It has always been my contention that, to grow, one must always be willing to question the status quo, look at new and different ways of doing things, and continually strive to improve. If you have a group of people sitting in a room and everyone is in lockstep and full agreement, you have a problem, since some people are not speaking up, for whatever reason. That is groupthink, and it results in stagnancy. You need to have those challenging views and that diversity of thought to see different perspectives and understand other points of view. While neither one may be completely right, there are pieces in each one worthy of consideration and which often prove beneficial. However, if you never have that conversation, you languish. And I never languished.

Expressing myself got me a lot of pushback from the boss or leader. Often this was because they weren't used to constructive criticism and were uncomfortable handling dissent. In those instances, I strived to take things professionally, not personally, and would always explain why I thought something was good for the business. Being more objective, with tangible references, was something which removed some of the objections—even biases. With persistence, it would usually pay off. In those instances where there was a disconnect or I felt I needed to make my case further, I would make every effort to arrange a one-on-one session to express my views. Often this worked, and sometimes it didn't, but at least I had the opportunity to express my views.

Speaking of one-on-one sessions and the need to communicate, I harken back to the first time I was given a management position with people reporting to me. There was one individual—a female but not African American—who stated she wouldn't report to someone like me, that is, an African-American female. She even went so far as to meet with the president of the company, stating she wouldn't report to me. To my surprise, I was called in to his office, told of the conversation, informed that "I" had a problem, and was told to "fix it." As a first-time manager, I was blindsided. I was the boss, she was the employee, and it wasn't supposed to be like that! However, I realized that this wouldn't be the last time something like this would happen, and I needed to be the bigger person. I approached the person and asked her to meet with me across the street for a cup of coffee. I started the conversation by saying, "I understand you don't want to report to me. What is it you don't like about me? What can I do to help you, as we are all in the same company? Your success and my success will help the company be successful, and isn't that what we want?"

Watching her reaction was transformational, and, at that moment, it dawned on me that, while I couldn't solve every problem or please every person, communication, empathy, and establishing common ground will get you a lot further than anything else. From that point forward, we had an excellent working relationship. She remains a friend to this day. And yes, I had similar experiences in the future, in which people expressed concern with reporting to a black female. Throughout my career, in almost every instance, having that conversation and establishing a relationship would bridge that gap and result in fruitful professional—and even personal—relationships. Of course, there were times when it didn't work. In those instances, I considered the source and never took it personally. Using the above examples, you may conclude that was my leadership style. Well, it was, and it wasn't. It was something I had to do based on the circumstances, as all leadership is situational. That is why I take exception to characterizations and catchphrases meant to portray someone as a certain type of leader. One that comes to mind is the whole Servant Leader movement. I always considered this a rather self-serving statement, especially when the people who call themselves that are usually the furthest from that concept. When I hear someone refer to themselves as a Servant Leader, I think to myself, *Who are you trying to convince?* If you care about the people you lead, you shouldn't need to announce that. And in what world is there nobility in being someone's servant? The phrase is catchy, somebody sold a book, and there it went! So, if you see yourself as Servant Leader or a Transformational Leader, for example, please disabuse yourself of those notions. You are simply a leader. You will act in the best interests of the business and the people, based on the prevailing circumstances and the personnel you are working with.

In tandem with these catchphrases concerning leadership, there is sometimes an accompanying training course you may attend to hone your leadership skills. However, if you are expecting to garner anything from one course, you need to recalibrate your expectations. Most of the leadership training today fails to develop leaders because "one and done" is not a recipe for true behavioral modification. You don't simply give a presentation, walk out, and expect it to be done. Here we need to rethink the concept of leadership in the arena of people development. It's the difference between a macro-view and a micro-view. The ability to impact behavior and improve performance is a continuum, which necessitates an ongoing coaching process. Whether these coaches are internal or external, or both, you need mentors who can help the developing leader understand how to unpack the knowledge and apply the leadership skills to the real world and the situations they will have to deal with.

Earlier in this chapter, I alluded to "follow-ship" as a requirement for developing your leadership, which it absolutely is. However, there is another issue which is sometimes overlooked—the issue of self-development and proficiency. Before one can lead others with confidence, you need that staunch belief in yourself and what you are about. In other words, it is difficult to lead others if you are unsure about yourself or insecure about your abilities. If *you* don't believe in you, how do you expect *others* to believe in you? That will manifest itself in many ways, and those in your charge will pick up on it. It may be subtle, but it's there and can undermine your ability to lead.

I observed this firsthand in many situations and came to the realization that, if I were to be accepted by others, I had to accept myself first and have an unwavering belief in my abilities. You have probably heard the saying that "planning and preparation are the keys to success." That certainly rings true and was central to my development. Some of this is due to my perception that, as a black female, there would be questions about me, my competency, my role, and my ability to perform and lead. I made a conscious and determined effort not only to understand but *master* anything and everything related to my position and understanding the business, inside and out. I admittedly am somewhat "OCD," and this mindset carried over to my job. I was determined not only to be prepared but to be *more* prepared. I would read, observe, ask questions, and dive as deep as possible into *all* aspects. No detail was too small, and no problem too big. If I didn't know the answer, I would find the answer. If I thought something could be a problem, I would construct plans—just in case; contingency planning is an important part of being prepared. I read case studies about the successes of businesses and—just as importantly—the failures. I looked at new and different ideas. Things don't always go the way we plan, and when that happens, you must be aware of what is happening, accept it for what it is, and adapt. I vowed never to be caught unaware and to maintain my composure, especially in a crisis. My preparation and willingness to address the problems—as opposed to running away from them—enabled me to develop a reputation for being able to turn "chaos into order." On numerous occasions, I became the go-to person, even if it wasn't within my department. This ingrained a strong sense of belief in myself, imbued a stronger belief in my abilities with others, and enhanced my ability to influence and lead.

Another component to this that must be practiced in tandem with the above is advocacy—advocacy for *yourself*. You must be your most ardent advocate. Too often we are told—and work under the assumption—that those who "go along, get along." *If you keep your nose to the grindstone, do your job, and work hard, you will be noticed and rewarded.* If you have that mentality and are waiting for someone or the company to take care of you, then you are in for a long wait. My approach was not to *wait* for something to happen but to *make* something happen. Too many people avoid conflict, but I did not shy away from it; I saw it as healthy. I was always engaged, would question the status quo, and take opposing positions for the sake of distilling the situation and the solution in the quest for new and different ways to improve something. A good analogy here is the classroom. In this regard, I was "always raising my hand," speaking up, and making my position clear. While this resulted in some people seeing me as difficult to work with, more people saw me for what I was—someone who had the courage to speak up and was earnestly interested in making good *better* and better *best*—for both the company and the people.

The experiences I've had in my leadership journey have been great. Meeting new people, researching new ideas and concepts, learning and training great minds and inspiring hearts—all of it has been memorable. Leadership is a continuum, and I have recently come to think differently about how I define leadership. As the environment evolves, so, too, must a leader evolve and adapt to be effective and relevant. Leadership today is not for the faint of heart and now encompasses a wider range of intertwined issues. Leaders must articulate a vision of the future state of the business or organization they lead. Leaders must assess the current environment—competition, regulatory, economic, and climate—and develop strategies to address the changing landscape. Leaders must clarify the reason the business or organization exists and effectively communicate that reason repeatedly to all stakeholders—clients, employees, and investors. If you strive to be an effective leader, you must do all these things—and more. Stay engaged, be transparent, and be open and willing to explore new ideas. And remember, along the way, you will have your share of disappointments and failures, but do not despair. Failure is proof that you are trying and is part of the cycle of success. Learn, adapt, and move on with a firm belief in who you are and what you are about.

I want to thank you for taking the time to get to know me and learn my views on leadership. I hope that, in this discourse, you picked up some ideas that will be useful to you on your leadership journey. As I alluded to several times, leadership is a journey, a continuum. I want to share something with you that I have on my desk in my office. This is advice that has served me well throughout my career; hopefully, it will provide guidance for you in your journey. I wish you all the best. Respectfully, Thomasina.

LESSONS I HAVE LEARNED

Love ME First!
Forgive Myself Faster!
Take Responsibility for the Good & Bad!
Check My Mindset: Doer or Dreamer?
What Am I Willing to Do to Grow?
What Am I Willing to Do to Get What I Want?

CHAPTER NINE

STEVEN MAYS

★ ★ ★ ★ ★

Steven was born in Charleston, West Virginia, into an Air Force family and is proud to be called a "military brat." He traveled the country and the world following his father during his career as an Air Force Sergeant. He graduated from the United States Naval Academy, having majored in math, and was selected for the Navy Nuclear Power program, despite one of the shortest interviews of all time with Admiral Rickover. He earned his gold dolphins aboard the USS Los Angeles (SSN–688), which was the lead ship in the Navy's fleet of attack submarines. His subsequent career involved safety and risk evaluations of nuclear power plants for the Idaho National Laboratory (INL), the civilian nuclear power industry in the United States and Canada, and government service with the Nuclear Regulatory Commission staff. He obtained a master's degree in electrical engineering via the GI Bill while working full time at the INL. He was awarded the Meritorious Service Award for his leadership at the NRC and graduated from the

Federal Executive Institute program "Leadership for a Democratic Society." He resides in Ashburn, Virginia, in the suburbs of Washington, DC, with his wife, Barbara. He has six children (including a set of triplets) and five grandchildren. He is passionate about storytelling and the subject of leadership. Steve believes that leaders are made, not born, and that teaching others how to lead is the most rewarding and vital occupation anyone can participate in. Steve can be reached at semcon@comcast. net to talk about leadership and swap sea stories. Of course, you must understand that fairy tales all begin with "Once upon a time," while sea stories always begin with "This is no BS." After that, they are identical.

★ ★ ★ ★ ★

LEADERSHIP IS THE ACT OF INFLUENCING OTHERS for their benefit in a cause greater than themselves alone. That is a terse but dense sentence. So, let's parse it some. Leadership is an act of influence, with two kinds of power at your disposal. One is the power of your power. The other is the power of your idea.

The first is illustrated by the following statement: "Show up for work at 0800 Monday through Friday, or you're fired." That is raw power—even tyranny, if you will—which is more often than not positional in nature. It is a threat of negative consequences for not delivering on an expectation solely determined by the leader. We all know this choice and probably have all used it at some point in life if we are parents. It has its place and is not always a bad idea. Use it sparingly, as it can engender discouragement and long-term distaste rather than generate a sense of common purpose and respect for all.

The second is illustrated by the following statement: "In order to win the conference tournament, we will need to practice twice a day for the next two weeks to improve our skills, implement our game plans, and be physically and mentally ready to compete." That is a statement of ideas that includes an assessment of where the group is, a delineation of where the team would like to be, and an indication of how the required effort would help achieve a common goal that everyone wants to achieve. This is the difference between leadership and forced compliance.

The ultimate goal of leadership is to make it possible for a group to achieve a goal that would be otherwise unattainable. An effective leader understands that the whole is greater than the sum of the parts. The leader knows that the combined efforts of a group of people enable achievement of a goal that none of them could reach on their own. The earliest civilizations formed tribes to fend off the dangers of the world and enhance the lives of the group. The need for cooperative action is the sole rationale for leadership.

Leadership is also a conscious choice to take action to influence others. The key words in that sentence are "choice" and "action." The idea that leaders are born to lead is ridiculous. We used to believe that the children of kings and queens were born to be kings and queens themselves. It is not a matter of birthright but a matter of choice. There isn't one leader who did not learn to be a better leader through their experience—and many times through trial and error. The more relevant question is *How can training, education, and experience improve a leader's capability to influence others in a particular field of endeavor?* It is true that some personality traits make it easier to be a leader and that individual style and character impact the ability to influence others. It is also true that some personality traits make it harder to be an effective leader. However, leadership is a choice to act. It is the choice that is the dominant factor—not the personality traits—in making you who you are.

The field of endeavor is also an important aspect to leadership. No one questions whether Mother Teresa or Patton would be a better Army leader. Similarly, no one questions which would make the better leader to help feed the poor. A leader, then, must have a skill set that includes both the nature of the endeavor and the ability to influence others in that field. This skill set is something which is developed over time, through training, experience, and commitment.

There is much discussion about which individual characteristics make a leader effective. However, I do not believe individual characteristics, in and of themselves, define a leader's effectiveness. But they *do* influence the manner in which leaders act.

Personal traits and style are often pointed out as key factors in leadership success. Consider some leaders who are widely accepted as particularly effective. Do they all demonstrate the same personal characteristics, or is there something they do that differentiates the great leaders from the lesser ones? If you look at it from that standpoint, you will be able to identify many great leaders with wildly different personal traits and styles. For example, did George Patton and Mahatma Gandhi share personal traits and style? What about Winston Churchill and Nelson Mandela or General Douglas MacArthur and Martin Luther King, Jr.? While their personal traits were different, what they had in common is that they were able to influence others to achieve more than they could achieve by themselves. It is the actions and the results, not the motivation, that separate better leaders from lesser ones.

Below is a simple diagram I developed in the book *The Power of 3: Lessons in Leadership*. I wrote the book to capture leadership lessons I learned along my leadership journey and to present them in a way that may benefit others in their leadership journey. The picture below is the Power of 3 Leadership Paradigm, which is a simplified visual presentation of those lessons. It is one of those things that will stick with you because, once you know something, it is difficult to not know it. For example, if I *order* you under pain of punishment not to think of an elephant, what is the first image that pops into your head? Exactly! The paradigm has three levels, which are discussed below: Foundation, Challenges, and Achievement. I hope this little picture proves useful to you.

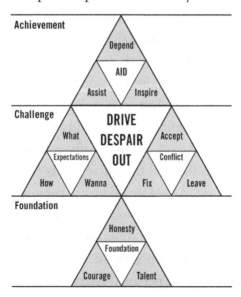

The Foundation is composed of three actions, all of which must be present for effective leadership:

1. *Honesty* is the ability to see the world and your situation the way it is—not the way you *want* it to be and not the way that it *could* be—but the *way it is*. This is important to the leader for knowing where they are and where they want to go. The followers must have a similar understanding for the leader to be effective. While personal characteristics like humility, curiosity, and critical thinking (among others) will make it easier for the leader to exhibit honesty, it is not the personal characteristic but the resulting achievement of honesty that is important. Long before I developed the Power of 3 Leadership Paradigm, I discovered that having a grasp on the circumstances that affected me and the people I wanted to lead was a huge factor in both my successes and my failures. I was often naïve and impulsive. That can be a dangerous combination. I had to learn to see things the way they *were* instead of the way I thought they *should be*. Youthful idealism often has that effect on people.

2. *Courage* is defined as the ability to overcome fear in order to take actions to benefit someone else without regard to the cost to yourself. It is the *action* that is important. As before, there are personal characteristics that will make it easier to take the action, such as empathy, self-deprecation, and selflessness. However, it is the resulting action that determines the effectiveness rather than the personal characteristics.

3. *Talent* involves the knowledge of how to do something, the skill to do something, and the perseverance to hone that skill to make it as good as you can make it. Personal characteristics like stubbornness, a drive to succeed, and openness to developing yourself will make it easier to maximize the talent. Once again, it is the *action* of becoming excellent in a particular field of endeavor that makes a leader more effective—not the factors motivating it.

An important sidenote regarding the Foundation. We spend an enormous portion of our time and energy working to develop our talent. Ask yourself this question: When was any significant failure in my personal or professional life due primarily to a lack of talent? I suspect the answer will be "Never." The cause of catastrophic failures of leadership usually resides elsewhere. However, these areas receive the least amount of attention in academic or formal training. So, we shouldn't be surprised when leaders fail catastrophically. It happens because we do not focus enough on *honesty* and *courage* in leadership development. We get the leaders we deserve based on the way we develop them. The old Native-American metaphor is that inside every person is a wolf that is destructive and evil and a wolf that is strong and helpful. The two wolves compete with one another to see which will dominate the person's soul. The answer? *The one you feed the most.*

As an example, everyone knows what their grades were in college or other educational setting. Everyone remembers their training activities. But who can remember their final grade on their *honesty final exam* or how they performed on their *courage capstone project?* These issues are critical to effective leadership, but they are seldom taught in academic or formal training. Any institution or training program for leadership should incorporate these principles into what they teach *and* how they operate. Any individual who strives to improve their leadership should keep these principles front and center at all times. You have to do this on your own because there are so few opportunities to do so in formal training.

While everyone has obstacles to overcome to lead successfully, most of these are self-imposed. I was no exception. I was slow in my ability to be realistic in my assessment of the world and my position in it. This is where *honesty* comes into play. You need to be honest with yourself, first and foremost. There were several shortcomings I needed to address, due to my bias and idealistic attitudes, which were not congruent with what was going on around me. For example, the importance of networking to enhance your career was something that took me a long time to appreciate. I had the view that networking was an obsequious effort to ingratiate oneself with others. I viewed keeping your head down and doing a great job was all that was needed to move up. It isn't. *Both* are needed, but my bias—even arrogance—against what I viewed as "kissing up" to others held me back. That was due to my inability to be *honest* about my situation.

Along the same lines, I thought that being correct about an issue was more important than how you presented the problem to others, particularly your seniors. I expected more of my seniors than I did of myself or my subordinates. Consequently, when they were in the wrong, I felt that making their errors known to them was important. It *was* important, but the *manner* in which it was presented was at least as important as the *content* of the concern. Being vocal about resolving problems is not sufficient. It is important to be vocal in an appropriate time and manner to allow the seniors the opportunity to evaluate your position without creating a barrier due to the manner in which it was presented. Challenging authority is inherently risky and requires a measure of tact and diplomacy that I lacked. My inability to realize that deficit in my approach to problem-solving is another case of me not being *honest* about my situation.

Going back to a point I made earlier, I can't recall any failures in my leadership journey that were primarily due to a lack of talent. Being honest about the world and your situation in it is particularly important in order to be an effective leader. It is hard to do and requires continuous updating of your worldview (or your "map," as Scott Peck refers to it). That requires critical thinking, humility, curiosity, and the ability to seek and accept advice regarding how to improve. The best leaders do it well—the worst, hardly at all.

The Power of 3 Leadership Paradigm includes a set of challenges that every leader has to overcome. These are dealing with unmet expectations, dealing with ethical conflicts, and dealing with despair. The most critical one for leaders is "Driving Despair Out." Despair is the opposite of love. Love is a powerful emotion that compels you to act for the benefit of others. Despair is a powerful emotion that *prevents* you from acting *at all*—for the benefit *or* detriment—of others. It is the shutdown button on your soul.

My epiphany about its importance came when I was stationed in Pearl Harbor on the attack submarine *USS Los*

Angeles. Captain Frank Kelso, who later became Chief of Naval Operations (CNO), was our squadron commodore, and his exemplary leadership and actions had a significant impact on my views of leadership and the importance of driving despair out of the organization. Two examples demonstrated his commitment to this concept.

While the ship was transiting to Pearl Harbor as a new home port, the wives and children were already there and dealing with housing, food, transportation, and a million other issues Navy families deal with while their spouses are at sea. The squadron had several vehicles with drivers assigned to assist the families who would gather at the squadron offices to coordinate services. Even though Captain Kelso was the "head honcho" of the squadron, whenever he would leave the offices for some activity elsewhere, he always checked to see if there were dependents in need of transportation before he left. He would provide rides in his personal car to anyone needing assistance before proceeding to his next activity. The impact on the dependents (and thereby on their spouses serving at sea) was tremendous. He didn't want anyone getting into despair due to their separation during the port change and went out of his way to prevent it.

During this time period, he would often go to sea in the ships under his command. During these sorties, his presence was visible, and his concern for the well-being of the crew was palpable. He would take the initiative, always asking the junior officers and chiefs how things were going for them and identifying ways he could help them achieve more professionally or personally. At the same time, I worked for a boss who thought that his job was to search out any imperfection, no matter how small, and demand immediate resolution. Over time, this approach of constant criticism of performance, never recognizing good performance, and exhibiting little concern for the well-being of the crew, led to a pall of despair. The despair generated by this approach was exactly opposite the approach of Captain Kelso. Observing these two styles and results in real time served to magnify the impact and importance of driving out despair, which, in my opinion, is the most critical element of successful leadership.

Looking back, as the real world kept intruding on my conceptual view of things, I became susceptible to despair and made too many decisions under despair that impacted my leadership trajectory. Some turned out fine—and some not so good. Decisions made in despair are gambles, at best. Recognize despair in yourself and others, and better results will surely follow. Failure is inevitable. Failing to learn from failure is a choice. It results in stagnation. I hate stagnation—it bores me.

From that time forward, I made it a point never to criticize anyone's performance unless I did two things. First, I would acknowledge what was right and good in the performance. Then I would make sure to cast whatever criticism followed in perspective to the overall goals so that the recipient of the criticism would understand that imperfect performance was not the "end of the world." It showed that correcting it would result in an improvement on a performance that was already heading in the right direction. My motto was "Progress, not perfection," and I found it to be very helpful in preventing despair from invading the work environment.

For missed expectations, there are three reasons they occur, which I group into *What*, *How*, and *Wanna*. In other words, it's because someone doesn't know what is expected, someone doesn't know how to meet the expectation, or someone just doesn't wanna meet the expectation. The responsibility for *What* and *How* lie with the leader, not the follower. The *Wanna* clearly belongs to the follower, but that is seldom the reason for missed expectations. More often, the leader fails to make clear the expectation or hasn't ensured that the follower knows how to meet the expectation. *How* includes more than just the technical skill to do a task. It also involves the time allotted, the resources provided, the support available, the prioritization of competing expectations, and the training/ experience necessary to do the tasks. It is a poor leader who proclaims, "It's my job to tell them what needs to be done and up to *them* to figure out how to do it."

When ethical conflicts arise, there are no winners. There are only options that are imperfect and decisions regarding which option you can tolerate. In this scenario, everyone gets hurt. The three options for dealing with ethical conflicts are *fix it*, *accept it*, or *leave it*. Unfortunately, there is another option that sometimes plays out and is a scenario you may have encountered. That is, do *not* fix it, do *not* accept it, and do *not* leave it. Instead, hang around, and bitch about it. You just pictured someone you know who matches this description. This option is a cancer to the person doing it and to everyone around them. There is only one cure for this cancer—excision.

The final level of the Power of 3 Leadership Paradigm is the Achievement Level. It consists of three parts that follow the acronym AID. "A" is for *assist*, "I" is for *inspire*, and "D" is for *depend*.

No leader can do everything themselves. They need others to perform. The leader's job is to assist them to perform. It really isn't that complicated, but it is amazing how many leaders forget that this is their responsibility.

Inspiration is the fuel that keeps the engine running. When each person in the organization understands the goal, the intention, and the steps needed to achieve the common goal, they can put their activities into proper perspective. The leader's job is to reinforce that understanding constantly, making sure that everyone understands the importance of their role in achieving the goal. Recognizing one's contribution to the performance inspires people to persevere through difficulties to achieve the common goal. It provides them with "ownership" and pride.

If a leader could do it all, there would be no need for followers. Therefore, it is imperative that leaders depend on others for success. Since it is human nature not to want to be blamed for failure, some leaders try to control as much of the activity as possible in order to have the best chance to create success. This is a false narrative. The leader *must* depend on others for success of the endeavor.

The concept of micromanagement is a direct result of leaders ignoring reality and trying to control everything. It doesn't work. The mistake too many leaders make is failing to realize that responsibility cannot be delegated, but authority can. If a leader is going to depend on others, they must have the authority to carry out the necessary actions. All too often, leaders maintain or even hoard authority, which impedes the ability of followers to act. It is an undeniable fact of life that leaders will be credited for success when they don't directly deserve it and blamed for failure when they don't directly deserve it. If you desire to be a leader, you must be able to accept this truth or get out of the leadership business.

In every endeavor, there are successes and failures, desired results and undesired results, and correct outcomes and errors. The leader's role is to focus the organization on moving forward to achieve a common goal. There is a difference between progress and perfection, and the focus of the leader needs to strike a balance between dealing with errors and successes along the way. Failure to do so distorts the vision for the followers and can lead to despair.

Leaders who believe that success is obtained only by focusing on avoiding failure will get what they focus on—failure. Followers need to know when they are going in the right direction, as it will reinforce their understanding of the common goals. It provides that dopamine "hit" that tells them they are making progress. Continuous harping on minor errors without perspective on the overall goal leads to a fear of making mistakes in the work environment. Deming, in his "Rules for Quality," listed, as a key element, "Drive fear out of the organization." The reasons are simple: fear leads to inaction, and attention to error without perspective leads to despair. The cycle becomes self-reinforcing, and failure becomes a self-fulfilling prophecy. Conversely, focusing on success in an appropriate perspective while fixing errors is the key to "driving out despair" in your organization. It is a factor that too many leaders fail to pay enough attention to. (By the way, the highest award for industrial quality in Japan is the Deming award, in recognition of the tremendous contributions he made to improving Japanese manufacturing capability.)

The Power of 3 Leadership Paradigm provides one way to look at the actions a leader must take to be successful. There are other leadership concepts that may do the same. Some may be better, some worse. The point is that every leader needs to develop their own leadership philosophy. There is no standard formula for successful leadership. It's not like physics where F=ma, and you just enter the values and "plug and chug" to get the answer. There are some general principles and concepts that seem to work in many cases. I like to borrow a concept from an excellent text on the subject, *It Starts with You*. You have to develop it, you have to nurture it, you have to test it, and you have to change it when necessary. To help you along that path are some actions that may be helpful:

1. **Develop a comprehensive concept of leadership.** It must encompass the full range of personal capabilities, challenges that you must deal with, and actions to take to fulfill your goal of influencing others to their benefit in pursuit of a goal none of you could achieve alone. There are thousands of books, classes, stories, lessons, and discussions on leadership that address aspects of leadership but few that address it in a comprehensive manner. Without a comprehensive approach, you will learn through trial and error—and plain dumb luck. It may make you a better leader, or it may not. Seek out a comprehensive philosophy of leadership that you can embrace.

2. **Write it down.** Admiral Hyman Rickover stated, "Nothing so sharpens the thought process as writing down one's arguments. Weaknesses overlooked in oral

discussion become painfully obvious on the written page." You have a leadership philosophy already. It is demonstrated by the way you act. Write it down, and then share it with others.

3. **Seek feedback.** Be self-deprecating and self-critical. Do not be afraid to improve your leadership philosophy as you learn from others and your own failures (and you *will* have them).

4. **Exercise your leadership model routinely.** Use your philosophy as a feedback mechanism to check on whether you are walking the walk as well as talking the talk. Nothing turns followers to despair faster than a leader who is hypocritical with regard to how followers are expected to act as opposed to how the leader acts. Evaluate your leadership regularly as you go. Use your written philosophy as a planning tool to address potential future issues. In other words, your leadership philosophy should be your road map for what you do today as well as your tool to evaluate how well you did yesterday.

5. **Get a mentor.** In fact, get as many as you can find to help you. Take as much information as they are willing to share, and determine where it can fit into your leadership philosophy. Then take action and use it.

6. **Make connections.** Your ability to exercise leadership at the highest levels will depend not only on how well you do with those you lead but also on how well you do with others who can influence your opportunities to lead. You are a valuable commodity. There is no shame in making your product known to others who could

benefit from using it. You do not have to compromise your personal humility or pride to do this, but you must make connections and network.

7. **Never, ever, give up.** Perseverance is a must for leaders. You cannot exercise control over all the outcomes, but you can always try to improve. None of us is perfect, but we can all learn, and we can all try to do better. Never, ever, give up.

The one thing I never doubted was that I would always have doubts as a leader. It comes with the territory. Letting your doubts paralyze you is the worst outcome. Being willing to risk and knowing you may fail is the hard part. You will fail. I guarantee it. But if you learn from failure, you will be better for it. The musical *The Man from La Mancha* said it best.

"And the world will be better for this.
That one man scorned and covered with scars,
Still strove with his last ounce of courage,
To reach the unreachable star."

I have no regrets about my leadership journey. There are things I could have done better and things I did extremely well. Some were noticed by others, and some were known only to me. Leaders can learn from failure and move on with a recognition that regret is just an opportunity missed. Regret is natural, but it has no practical purpose except to motivate learning. As long as learning is occurring, there is no useful purpose for regret. What is done is done. What is important is what you are about to do next. That is why the greatest leadership lessons are in the old oral histories and old stories like *Aesop's Fables*. They serve the purpose of reminding us of how failures occur so that we can potentially avoid them. They also remind us of how successes occur so that we can emulate them. Most of all, leadership is about choosing to act. So, whatever you do, choose to act.

CHAPTER TEN

DARALEE BARBERA

★ ★ ★ ★ ★

Dr. Daralee Barbera, EdD, CFP®, CMFC®, ChFC®, CPBC®, CLF®, is passionate about the importance of financial planning, personal and business development, and the critical role of leadership. She is a certified business coach, international speaker, professor, author, and consultant. Dr. Barbera holds an EdD in Leadership and Organizational Change from The University of Southern California, a BA in Mathematics (summa cum laude), and an MA in Secondary Education from California State University Long Beach. Dr. Barbera is adjunct professor in the MSM and MSFP/MBA programs at The American College and California Lutheran University, respectively. Daralee is a veteran of the financial services profession, retiring as Managing Principal after a distinguished 34-year career at Waddell and Reed. She was the Executive Vice President of GAMA International. She is President of Diversified Professional Coaching (DPC) LLC. Dr. Barbera has co-authored two books: Women Matter: The Why and How of Gender Diversity in

Financial Services *and* What You Can Do . . . When You Can't: 21 Days to Personal Success. *Her doctoral dissertation addressed Financial Literacy for Women and the Role of Financial Education. As well as having served on The American College's Board of Trustees, she is Past President of the GAMA International Board of Directors, past "Woman of the Year" for WIFS (Women in Insurance and Financial Services), was named as one of the "20 Women in Insurance You Need to Know" in 2013 by Life Health Pro, is Chairman Emeritus of FPA Orange County, and serves as an advisor for The American College Northwestern Mutual Granum Center for Financial Security. She belongs to FINSECA, NAIFA, FPA, and WIFS. She is on the Speaker Bureau for Life Happens, FINESCA, and DPC.*

★ ★ ★ ★ ★

THE LEADERSHIP TOOLBOX

To SAY THAT I AM PASSIONATE ABOUT THE CRITICAL ROLE that leadership plays would be an understatement. Leadership affects all of us on a daily basis, whether we are the leader or the follower. The impact of good leadership can have a positive domino effect, with global impact, lasting for generations. Similarly, poor leadership, ineffective leadership, or misguided leadership can be disastrous, touching far beyond the moment where it occurred. A "Leadership Toolbox" is helpful for anyone working on growing their skills as a leader or future leader. Many helpful tools are covered in this chapter, including inclusive leadership, de-skilling, goal setting, and factors conducive to growing leadership skills. A good Leadership Toolbox can take you to the next level in your journey as a leader.

LEADERSHIP TODAY

What is leadership? Are you a leader? In fact, the odds are high that you are a leader, as someone likely reaches up to you for your knowledge, skills, experiences, and motivation. You are probably also a follower, as there is someone you reach up to in the same fashion. Leadership can be tricky to identify, as it is dynamic and in motion, involving leaders, followers, and the setting you are in. What does it look like, and would you know it if you saw it?

Leadership today includes defining factors that continue to evolve. Understanding that leadership definitions have changed over time can help to inform where some of the notions of leadership originate. Some of the themes of yesterday were more narrowly defined and included the exterior traits of a leader—if they looked the part—as well as how a leader exerted dominance, control, and power. Contemporary leadership consists of many things and is an interaction involving the setting, the follower-ship, and the leadership. Factors that contribute to defining leadership in action include trustworthiness, values, core beliefs, positivity, teamwork, influence, communication, authenticity, emotional intelligence, self-awareness, decision-making prowess, confidence, competence, and results orientation. The effective leader of today may be unassuming and a skillful questioner and listener. They may use fewer words but speak to inform and inspire, in contrast to command and control. Leadership today is an open door for the many, rather than for the few.

ALWAYS A SCHOOL DAY

Education is the centerpiece of my frame of reference for leadership. I started my professional life as a teacher at the high school and college level, with a BA in Math and an MA in Secondary Education. Most of my career was in the profession of Financial Planning, where I spent 30 years as a Managing Principal. I retired from financial planning to pursue business coaching and graduate-level teaching of Leadership, Management, and Financial Planning after earning my Doctorate in Leadership and Organizational Change. How people learn, how they build knowledge and skills, how they apply their knowledge and skills, as well as their motivation, is my personal framing. It's that window that I look through to see and understand life, where every day is a school day, as there is so much yet to be learned. In a learning environment, it is normal, and expected, to question and build skills to find answers. The educational setting creates a good environment for growing and developing leadership, as it promotes learning, growing, sharing, helping, and working together.

I became interested in leadership early in life, and the school setting was formative. Growing up, I was busy and involved in many activities on and off of my campuses. I had opportunities to take on leadership roles, which I happily accepted. When I realized that I had "followers," I took the responsibility seriously. Quickly figuring out that followers count on leaders to "get it right," I worked to do the best job I could to lead well, working with other peer leaders, teachers, and mentors. Leadership is not a solo sport; it involves others as participants, and, therefore, a team approach defines leadership for me. Leadership was not about me getting things done alone, but together, with, and through others, by sharing responsibilities for tasks, skills, and results. "Together is better, and solo is a no-go" has been one of my favorite leadership mantras. It is the interaction of followers, the setting, and the leader that create the stage for leadership to happen. Required as well are skillful, capable, trustworthy leaders to serve as good role models to create an encouraging environment to grow more leaders.

DE-SKILL TO GROW OTHERS
Leadership, to me, has always been about helping others to attain personal and professional growth. Whether a client is defining or accomplishing their life's goals and dreams, or a manager is working to inspire their team to that next level of success, the starting point is a common one. It starts with individuals knowing themselves, their strengths, and the frame they are working in. To get from where you are now to where you want to go usually requires others, particularly in the world of leadership.

As a manager, building a solid leadership bench was a priority. The greater the organizational depth, the further an organization can get. The most helpful concept for bench-building is "de-skilling." This means to share your load with others, teaching them new tasks so that they can build skills and potentially grow as future leaders. Part of my rule set here is to identify any tasks that I do that someone else could do instead. I ask myself if these are tasks that "only I" can do. If so, then these are the tasks I retain. All other tasks should be shared with team members who have the potential to do the job. They have to be shown how and allowed proper time to build the skills, but it is important to have a succession plan for each organizational task. It is an investment of time and patience to train others, but it is worthwhile to build a bench of future leaders.

I spent several early years as a manager not realizing how critical it is to "de-skill." Very late one night, I was working at the office, catching up on the day's work, and I realized that, even if I worked straight through the night, I still could not accomplish all the tasks on my desk. This was clearly an unsustainable spot to be in. I accepted that I needed help. The solution was to share these responsibilities with my team. I had goals that exceeded my capacity to obtain alone. "If you're going to grow, you have to let go" became my reality check and another favorite saying. If someone else can do a task, let go of it, and grab the next thing that no one else can do but you. This is how we grow leaders—by sharing and caring about improving the team members' capacity to be of service and to contribute to the team.

Growing others requires that leaders pay it forward. It involves tapping that next generation of potential leaders on the shoulder and telling them that you nominate them to take the next step. You'll need to encourage them that they can do this and that you'll show them the way. This is an opportunity to build up trust in your leader-follower relationship. The task or job that you are sharing was important enough that you were personally completing it, so getting the job done successfully is the only option. Success is encouraging and confidence building for developing leaders. For myself, many of my personal milestones were as a result of leaders I trusted tapping me on the shoulder and inviting me to take a step in a direction that I had not planned on.

Your promise to support those you tap with resources for success is a fair trade for their reciprocating commitment to accept the task. It takes a confident leader to share their path with others. This handoff benefits leaders, not only by expanding organizational capacity, but by gaining personal time for you that can be spent on other things. Time is often our most precious currency. Just an added hour a day back on your calendar, based on a 40-hour work week, generates an additional 6.5 weeks into your schedule each year. Envision how that time can be invested back into your business and life.

3 Cs FOR INCLUSIVE LEADERSHIP

Today's leaders have many challenges. Intrinsic to the times, the challenge of 2020 and 2021 was the COVID-19 pandemic. The logistical stresses it brought modified how people live their lives, frequently creating more personal time spent at home and less time spent with others. The pandemic has shown us many things, but one thing that has been reinforced with heightened visibility is that who someone is matters a lot. How people self-identify matters. Who they are, as a unique team member, matters. And, that people want to be included and to contribute to solutions matters. These are areas for leadership development that serve us well as skills that resonate now and in an uncertain future.

Inclusive leadership has never been more important. This is leadership that creates camaraderie, brings people together, and recognizes and celebrates individuality. When we search for it in traditional leadership textbooks, we find leadership types such as Transformational, Situational, Transactional, Servant, and Charismatic, to name a few. Inclusive leadership is not likely to be found. Inclusive Leadership is a contemporary fundamental concept and skill for leaders. The time for Inclusive leadership is now. There are three solid areas of focus for Inclusive leaders: Community, Communication, and Connectivity. These are 3 Cs for Inclusive leadership.

Community is not just a place to go. People like to belong, and they seek community, but the pandemic created isolation. Communities were traditionally defined by geography, but today the power of community extends beyond a neighborhood or physical border. Shared beliefs, cultures, values, causes, and skills can all define community. Community is interconnectedness, a belonging, a shared ownership, and responsibility. Today, leaders can go to the community of another and belong instantly, virtually connecting into homes and personal spaces like never before. Technology has allowed leaders access into communities that they were previously not a part of, or even nearby. Many will follow leaders for the community that the leader fosters. Inclusive Leadership builds community. Community is where we connect.

Connectivity is engagement fostered by community. Building connection through meetings is a powerful tool for the Inclusive Leader. From in-person meetings, whether individual or group, to using Facetime and Zoom or other distanced connections, we are surrounded by engagement opportunities. The interconnectedness of the team, whether in the same space or not, provides for higher organizational performance, working hand in hand with foundational skills for conducting effective meetings.

Communication is key to connection. Without excellent communication skills, we are operating in a deficit, both personally and professionally. Communication is not always easy and can result in unintended messaging. It can be complicated, but it's a foundational skill for inclusive relationships. Leaders with good communication skills can be better resources, educators, and motivators, and can better evidence their commitment and care for their team.

Communication has three components: the sender, the message, and the receiver. When a sender encodes and sends a message, and when a receiver decodes the message, we have communication. It sounds pretty simple. When communication goes right, it has to do with the execution of these three steps. Lack of critical skills in these areas can adversely impact communication and inclusion.

Effective listening is a part of the inclusive-communication equation. A leader who asks questions, who is an active listener, and who is targeted in their responses is a leader who can effect change more impactfully. I have always trained that the ratio of listening to speaking should be about two to one, the same ratio as ears to mouths, whereas some recommend as high as three or four to one. Simply, *listening more than we speak* can be a very effective and useful skill.

I can recall specific instances where some of the greatest leaders that I have ever worked with asked me specific questions, listened intently to my answers, and then responded with comments that were specific to what I had said. This was very directive and impactful for me. In some instances, they were career-changers. Leaders who apply refined questioning and listening skills acknowledge the follower and give recognition to them as an individual, producing more meaningful communication, which is more actionable, as it is specific. This illustrates the power of Inclusive Leadership and its targeted potential to facilitate change.

GOALS

Evaluating leaders based on performance is what keeps most leaders in their leadership seats. Setting and accomplishing goals is a critical skill set for leaders. Leaders do not cross the finish line solely on their own but rely on others to get them there. When I first became a manager in the early '80s, a common concept was to "manage" people to obtain results. This approach was very against my grain, and I instead "coached" for results. Coaching is a focus on a person, not a focus on a thing or a problem, helping them to accomplish results based on leveraging their strengths and skills. Professional goals a leader sets must integrate with personal goals, as, for goals to be effective, they must resonate with the whole person. This is where the "why" of a goal needs to be clear, to the leader and to followers. The "why" should fit with core values, both professionally and personally. We are but one person, and, when we show up for work, we don't leave the personal part at home.

Why do we set goals? We set goals to create positive change—change that is the cornerstone of growth. Growth comes from setting and attaining goals for change, noting that change is tough for most people. Change is a departure from the current and a transition to a new future, often feeling like going from the known to the unknown. This requires trust in the leader. Trust survives well in an inclusive environment, where people feel that their leader really understands them and that they understand their leader. This creates a safe space for personal and professional transitions, which impacts successful change and goal attainment.

The best way to get to successful change across the organization is to have a deliberate goal-setting process that is simple, actionable, repeatable, and meaningful. Business goals are often public goals and, as such, have even more of an imperative to be transparent and motivational, and result in purposeful change. The "why" of the goal is the real driver for the team, followed by the importance of the "how" and the "what." As a leader's goals are an aggregation of the team goals bubbling up for a collective result, the leader's goals should be communicated to the team and the team kept informed as to their progress. It took me years to learn this. I was fortunate to be in a Leadership Study Group, where I saw the success that other leaders experienced with the collective buy-in that public goal tracking brings.

Successful goal-setting skills are something that leaders cannot live without and can be found in the first book that I co-authored, *What You Can Do . . . When You Can't: 21 Days to Personal Success*. The book takes a positive approach to setting and attaining personal and professional goals and demonstrates how to use a "simple as 1-2-3" step process. I have presented this process to many thousands of leaders globally. Focusing on the premise that, in every "I Can't" there is an "I Can," we focus on what can work and apply the three simple steps for goal setting—Evaluate, Formulate, and Act.

★ The **Evaluate** step starts with understanding where you are currently and where you want to go.

* The **Formulate** step looks at how to bridge the gap and how to accomplish the goal. What process will we use? What is the strategy, and what are the tactics?

* The last step is to **Act** and get to work on executing the plan. How long will it take to get there? How will we know when we've arrived? What is the most direct route from point A to point B?

In addition to the "simple as 1-2-3" step process, the concept of "21-day goals" is presented in the book. When goals are set in realistic 21-day increments, goals are more manageable. This creates a recipe for success, as when goals are smaller, their likelihood of being accomplished increases. Annual goals are divided into monthly goals that are attainable in 21 days, with a plan for assessment. If only one goal is set for each month, that equates to 12 new goals accomplished every year, 60 new goals every 5 years, 120 new goals every 10 years, and so on. Experiencing tangible results is inspirational and perpetuates motivation for growth.

The answer to the question, "What would need to happen for this to be your best year ever—professionally and personally?" is likely based on a result of some sort. Starting with the end in mind is an effective approach for goal setting, as your destination will be clear. When you arrive at your destination, what does success look like for all of the involved parties—for the leader, for the follower, for the organization, for the project? When evaluating your results, identify what went well. Consider what results were less than satisfactory. What changes are needed for next time to enhance success?

Did you as the leader, and the team, do the best job possible based on your knowledge, motivation, and the influences of the setting? Are there areas for skill development, and, if so, how will that be accomplished? A results-based approach for goals is as "simple as 1-2-3" and applies well the three-step process of Evaluate, Formulate, and Act.

IN CONCLUSION

Leadership matters and touches the lives of many. A Leadership Toolbox with just the right tools can determine a leader's success. Applying just one of these tools can ignite meaningful change. Change often starts with just one: One extra degree of heat makes steam, one extra atom of hydrogen makes water, and one good leader can transform lives. Indeed, one small change or just one special leader, can motivate and inspire accomplishments for generations. Be that leader!

CHAPTER ELEVEN

JOHN STUFFLEBEEM

★ ★ ★ ★ ★

John "Boomer" Stufflebeem is a former professional football player and retired U.S. Navy admiral. He learned the value of elite teamwork and skills in the NFL and leadership from the cockpits of aircraft-carrier jet fighters. He led as a commander of troops in every major military operation from 1994 to 2007. Additionally, he carried the nuclear "football" for President George H.W. Bush as a Military Aide in the White House before taking command and leading in combat in the Balkans and Southwest Asia. He was in the Pentagon as a war planner when the USA was attacked on 9/11 and became the face and voice to the world on radio and television from the Pentagon of operations in Afghanistan in response to those attacks. "Boomer" learned the tenets of successful leadership under fire through firsthand experience. His business today in crisis management as owner of the NJS Group, LLC, and Executive/Business Coaching of Diversified Business Coaching, LLC, is based on more than thirty years' experience and expertise in leading under extreme stress. He is highly sought by corporations, companies (public and private), NFL clubs, athletes, and executives to improve their leadership and performance by a factor of two-and-one-half times. John is a lifetime member of the National Football League Players Association and is a Certified Professional Business Coach. He is widely engaged as a consultant, advisor, mentor, coach, and speaker on the intricacies of elevating leadership during crises.

★ ★ ★ ★ ★

LEADERSHIP IS OWNERSHIP OF THE SUCCESS of the enterprise. A leader, first and foremost, is responsible for successful outcomes. A leader defines himself or herself by the style of leadership given to those the leader works for and works with. A leader accepts responsibility and full accountability for their well-being and the outcome. The style in which the leader goes about doing this is defined by how the leader earns and gains respect and following.

When I was about to take my first command in the Navy of an aircraft-carrier fighter squadron that was soon to go into combat, I was given some great advice from my soon-to-be boss. He pointed out to me that I would make a difference in a number of lives whether I would ever know it or not. He said, "Count on this—you will save somebody's life, someone's career, and even a marriage. And never forget how much I am counting on you to do your job right." To this day, twenty-six years later, I marvel at his prescient remarks. I am still taken aback when someone from that squadron contacts me and tells me that I saved their life, their career, and/or even their marriage. It still takes my breath away. I never forgot that weighty nugget of leadership and have consistently passed it on ever since. It is a factual definition of leadership—you are responsible for the outcomes and will make a difference, even if you never know about it.

It is certainly true that some people exhibit leadership characteristics from an early age and excel at nearly everything. However, I refrain from using the phrase "natural-born leader" when characterizing someone's leadership ability. While there may be traits or characteristics resident within someone that enable them to become effective leaders, it is not these traits that make them effective leaders, nor is it simply someone merely rising to the occasion. Instead, it is the culmination of time, environment, and their experiences. These experiences, particularly when having to endure adverse circumstances—and even failure—are of incalculable value as they create learning and growing opportunities that will enable them to cope with and adapt as necessary in the future. While I didn't realize it at the time, the more severe the circumstances, the greater the opportunity for growth and success. These "crucibles" or trials by fire help someone develop their leadership in several ways by doing the following:

1. They help to create courage, which is the ability to conquer fear and succeed.
2. They build confidence in one's ability by stretching their limits and defining new ones.
3. They gather wisdom through circumstances that deliver knowledge and experience, which is far more valuable than prestige or enthusiasm.

One of the experiences I had for which I am forever grateful is the honor of working directly for President George H.W. Bush, or Bush #41, for nearly two years while he was in the White House. I was able to observe, firsthand, how he rose to the challenges posed by Manuel Noriega, the dictator of Panama, and later, by the Iraqi invasion of Kuwait by Saddam Hussein. His leadership during these two crises was impressive as well as instructive, to the point where books have been written about how adroitly he handled these two crises. Suffice it to say he did not have all the answers, but he did rise to the occasion and to a leadership level that imbued confidence in all those around him and assured success in both operations. Later, he noted that his success as a leader stemmed directly from what he was taught from those he worked with along the journey of his life, including his time in the military. And he never stopped learning, as he was a "made leader" and a terrific example for all of us to learn from as well, since we, too, never stop learning.

If you were to look at the desired characteristics for an effective leader, these three are at the top of my list—gratitude, integrity, and resilience. These are not only important but absolutely necessary. In combination with these, I have found these additional characteristics or skills to be the ones that are most valuable as it relates to getting things done in the right way, at the right time:

1. Vision: The ability to see and articulate an outcome.
2. Focus: The ability to stay strategic and not get bogged down in the operational or tactical decision-making process.

3. Perseverance: The ability to stick with it and never give up, regardless of the circumstances, pressures, or time.

4. Humility: The willingness always to give credit to and for what others do and accept accountability for those things that don't go as planned or for those people who do not perform well.

5. People skills: The ability to inspire others, see their potential and nurture them, have empathy for others, and be willing to always put others' needs ahead of your self-interest.

6. Communication: The ability to listen, ask good questions, and never assume others know what you are thinking, to always under-react, exuding confidence and exhibiting a calm demeanor, and to simplify, clarify, and focus on the right outcomes.

I had the distinct honor to command organizations and fighting units in combat at four different levels, and it still humbles me to think that I was entrusted with the lives of so many people. These ran the spectrum of a fighter squadron as a Navy Commander to a numbered fleet as a Vice Admiral. With each experience, I had opportunities to closely observe those I worked for, worked with, and who worked for me. I could see standout characteristics in all three groups, some of which I admired and others I abhorred. Every person, organization, and unit I commanded were all instructive in making me a better leader by understanding what to emulate, what to improve, and what to avoid or prevent. I learned that, at every level of leadership, the values I held and espoused determined what characteristics others would see in me and that the example I set would be instructive for them. I also realized I had to be self-aware of and sensitive to what characteristics I wanted them to observe and that I needed to be disciplined and consistent in doing so. From that, they would learn, as I did, how to make others better leaders by setting the example, making themselves better leaders, and opening and closing it all with gratitude.

If I were to name what people or experiences were most beneficial in helping me to develop my leadership, I would put them into one category. This would be the leaders I observed under extreme stress, often accompanied by the need to make grave decisions. Observing how these leaders conducted themselves during these times of crisis and the processes they used were the most influential experiences in enabling me to become the most effective leader possible. I realized I had to be mentally strong and disciplined and that I had to ignore the fear of failure and the accompanying fight-or-flight emotion of panic when severely challenged. Like fire strengthens steel, the more I was exposed to it, the more resilient and confident I became—all of which enabled me to develop competence and effectiveness as a leader, especially in times of crisis, when a leader is the difference between success and failure, and life and death.

These experiences underscore the importance of two firm convictions or tenets any leader must master: Never go it alone, and never believe *you* are the answer to all the problems. As an example, when I commanded a fighter squadron during combat in the Balkans, I had a junior pilot who lost his confidence, which became a problem within his flight section and for many of the other officers. The results could have been tragic, given that we were dealing directly in life-and-death operations. I realized this was not something I could fix myself and that it would require a team effort to get him back up on his horse and support his workmates in the manner they depended on. I then went to his closest peers, his immediate supervisor, and a trusted confidant outside the squadron and asked for their help.

We put together our assessment and developed a plan of action with recommendations. Prior to doing this, I also ran our plan by my immediate superior to get the benefit of his experience and secure his review and sign-off. Once this was done, we approached the junior pilot and sat down with him. We reviewed our plan and recommendations, and went over the benefits and penalties of buying in to the plan. When we first approached him, he did act somewhat surprised, but in actuality, he was relieved. It was apparent he desperately needed our guidance and support. Knowing there were others who cared about him and had his back, so to speak, was a source of inspiration and strength for him. During the meeting, I thought I saw tears well up in his eyes—they might have been in mine, for that matter. In any event, it worked, and, after that meeting, with a plan and support system in place, he turned things around and got back on that horse. He became one of our strongest aviators and officers; to this day, he is performing in an exemplary manner.

As a leader, you will face a number of challenges, with overcoming the fear of failure being your biggest challenge. Invariably, the next is not trusting in your own judgment and not following your instincts alongside the data needed to help make good decisions. I would submit that the third is losing focus. Here you need to focus on what is most important, which is the goal, and not lose focus on the big picture by getting pulled down into the tactical weeds. Ethics should not be a problem, and, admittedly, we all have a few ethical problems when it comes to following rules and such. However, when it comes to your moral compass, compromise, skirting the rules, taking shortcuts, and not staying true to your value system and those of your organization cannot and should not be tolerated.

However, the above issues notwithstanding, the biggest challenge I had to face as a leader was my ego. Perhaps it was my inner drive, my athletic background, or my need to compete and win that spawned this, but at first, I really had issues accepting when I was wrong and admitting it to others. At successive levels of command leadership, too often I found myself feeling "I can do this better than they can" or words to that effect, which did not help us reach our goals. Fortunately, as I became more senior and more practiced, I was keeping my ego in check and came to the realization that acceptance of wrongdoing is not a weakness but a strength and a learning experience. I didn't have all the answers, nor did I need to have all of them, since it is the collective input and efforts of the team that determine success—not one person. Consequently, over time, I put my ego aside; the leadership journey quickened, and, with it, the accompanying success and fulfillment.

Any mention of challenges would not be complete without addressing obstacles, which are different from challenges. Whereas a challenge is a response to a situation and is something you can actively deal with and address, an obstacle is something that serves to impede progress, to block an action, or prevent something from being implemented. In many respects, everything is an obstacle to leadership in some way or another, and there are myriad obstacles you will encounter. In these instances, you have to deal with them straight on or chart a completely different path or strategy. The obstacles I had to overcome to help create success included having a toxic boss, taking over underperforming units, having too many naysayers, damage, injury, deaths (including suicides), too few resources, too little guidance, unreasonable and/or unattainable expectations, lack of trust, not creating high-enough standards, not forcing simplicity, not providing clarity, losing focus due to minutiae, failing to appreciate the effects and impacts of my leadership, answering the question asked, and figuring out what was most important, among others. After reading this, you may say "Is that all?" which is a tongue-in-cheek remark on my part. The point I am trying to make is that, throughout your leadership career, there will always be a host of issues or obstacles that will stand in your way. There always have, and always will be, as rarely do things go easy or go well. It is in these instances that a leader's mettle is tested. And here, as Hannibal said to his men when crossing the Pyrenees—elephants and all—you have to "Find a way or make one."

None of us are without fault, and we all make mistakes. In retrospect, these are the biggest mistakes leaders make. Being cognizant of these issues will help you avoid the pitfalls and consequences which follow these mistakes.

1. **Loss of focus.** The biggest mistake many leaders make is losing sight of the strategic imperative or big picture. No one else in an organization is as responsible for the success, the outcome, and the vision for that

organization than its leader. Once leaders are drawn down into their comfort zones of the day-to-day tactical or operational issues is when focus for *the main thing* is lost.

2. **Arrogance.** Believing they know all and have all the answers. Many leaders mistakenly assume that, since they are in charge, they must have all the answers—why else would they have been put there? Furthermore, they often feel compelled to offer their solutions and advice or give directions when they rarely have all the requisite information to make the best decisions.

3. **Insecurity.** Believing they cannot be seen as making poor decisions or making mistakes. It is much more empowering to let people know of your concerns, your doubts, and your questions, and let people help you make good decisions. It builds credibility faster, which is one of the key fundamentals to building trust. Allow yourself to be and be seen as vulnerable. Practicing this in increasing effort beats down insecurity.

4. **Not setting an example.** To be worthy of being followed, a leader must have his or her people's trust. To build trust, one must give it and have credibility. To gain credibility, a leader must match actions to words, be willing to back his or her people, and accept accountability for their shortcomings. A leader must always be moral, knowing the difference between right and wrong, and do the right thing, regardless of the consequences. At all times, the leader should conduct him- or herself in a manner beyond reproach and in an exemplary manner that continually reinforces these points.

5. **Not trusting their instincts.** Judgment is the ability to make considered decisions or come to sensible conclusions. It is the result of a blend of experience, wisdom, and instinct. It is important to "trust your gut" and not disregard it out of hand. If it doesn't sound right, doesn't feel right, and doesn't smell right, chances are it isn't right. Many is the time leaders have lamented, "I should have trusted my instincts."

When asked what my leadership style is, I always characterize it as "work for my people." I learned early on that, if I did a good job of taking care of those I was responsible for, they, in turn, would take good care in getting the job done. People come to work believing they can do a good job but wonder whether they will be supported. They are already motivated, so it is incumbent on a leader to build on that rather than tear it down. Having said that, there is no one best style of leadership, and I really don't pay much mind to all the terminology and hype bandied about concerning styles. It takes a variety of skills applied at the right times, to the right individuals, in the right way, to work best. It is also important to bear in mind that leadership is an art, even as it is studied as a science. And as we have all seen, leadership training is a big business, as there are countless seminars and courses out there. However, to really learn leadership and how to effectively lead, there is only one way and no better teacher than experience.

With the above statement, you are now probably wondering, *What can I do to develop my leadership skills?* I would be remiss if I did not offer specifics and recommendations. As you have probably seen, I have a penchant for organizing and grouping things, either by numbering them or using bullet points. It is simply something I have picked up over time that I have found to be quite effective in communicating to ensure clarity, understanding, and retention. So, for those of you who are serious about developing your leadership skills, here are six action items.

1. **Watch and listen.** Find an environment where leadership is practiced, not given lip service, and continually reinforced. Observe those leaders you respect; mentally catalog best practices (those things you like about a leader), what he or she does right, or even what you deem wrong, for that matter.

2. **Ask good questions.** The best way to start is by de-personalizing any question. Take the "who" out of it, and focus your words on the "what." You will be much more impressed with or at least appreciative of the responses.

3. **Leap!** Be willing to go for it and not fear failure, unless it derails your company or hurts someone. Failure will teach one more about leadership than all the schooling that can be had. Remember—there is a leap of faith in just about anything you do, so take that leap.

4. **Seek opportunity.** Be willing to go after and accept any leadership challenge. The challenge, resultant experience, and travails will make you smarter, better, and faster. Remember my earlier analogy about steel and fire. The tougher the challenge, the better.

5. **Learn to follow.** You can't really lead until you can empathize with those you are leading. There is no better way than to have been in their shoes at one time

and reflect back on what motivated you, what didn't motivate you, whom you admired, and so forth. It also gives you a good dose of humility, which is a necessary ingredient to add to your leadership makeup.

6. **Find a mentor.** This should be someone you can trust to give you good advice and should be outside of your direct-report chain. Remember, a mentor is not someone to necessarily guide you but more to coach you, by helping to lead you in the right direction so that you make the very best decisions.

After reading my recommendations, you may be wondering if they work and why they are in this order. These recommendations come from my own experience, based on what I have done, and in that order. How did this happen? In my teens, there was always something inside me that, even to this day, I cannot articulate, but that spurred me to wanting to excel and be respected. Here, the leadership aspect or subject was something that always got my attention. While I was competitive in sports and did fairly well, as I was able to play collegiately and even managed to make it to the NFL, I was enraptured by the vision and impact of those in leadership positions whom people looked up to, and I wanted to be like them. The military academies got my attention, and specifically, the United States Naval Academy. I was convinced this venerable institution and the entire experience would help me develop and hopefully become a leader that others would respect and emulate. I even attended a military-college-preparatory school in the hope that I would gain admittance. Fortunately, I did, and my time in Annapolis forged and strengthened my leadership skills. I learned to follow and understand the value of teamwork over self. I developed further discipline and restraint in a very strenuous and stressful environment and learned to persevere. I began to understand the processes involved for developing the competence and confidence to be successful, and how to focus by gaining clarity and having perspective. Later, as a career military officer, I was able to build on this foundation of leadership throughout my life's work.

Before I sign off, I will cover one question that people often ask me, and that is "Knowing what you know now, what would you change?" My response here is that I would not change a single thing. However, there are four areas where I could have done better, and you can as well, if you do the following. One, when making decisions—assuming you have the luxury of time—make better decisions with more time, more thought, and more teamwork. Two, try to develop as good an understanding as possible of what someone is about, why they are acting a certain way, or even how you view them. Things always aren't what they appear to be, so take the time to dig a little deeper. Three, *pay attention!* Pay closer attention to everyone and everything around you, including other leaders, those under your command, and the operative details. The best answers, the best solutions, and the best courses of action are always there *if* you can free yourself to see them. Four, recognize leadership is a never-ending journey of experience and learning. As the song goes—"I'm waiting for my real life to begin," and I believe my greatest leadership challenges and best opportunities are in front of me.

CHAPTER TWELVE

MORDECAI BROWNLEE

★ ★ ★ ★ ★

Dr. Mordecai Ian Brownlee currently serves as the President of the Community College of Aurora in Aurora, Colorado. Founded in 1983, CCA is a Hispanic-Serving Institution with campuses in Aurora and Denver. Previously, Dr. Brownlee served as the Vice President for Student Success at St. Philip's College, the only college in the nation federally designated as both a Historically Black College (HBCU) and an Hispanic-serving institution, located in San Antonio, Texas. Mordecai also served as an adjunct professor at Morgan State University School of Education & Urban Studies and the University of Charleston School of Business and Leadership, where he taught business management, human resources, social justice, and community-college leadership. In addition, he is a higher-education columnist for EdSurge. Dr. Brownlee is a leader in a number of national, statewide, and district/ system initiatives that empower the academic pathways of students and promote student success. Those initiatives include the guidedpathway model, strategic-enrollment management, Baldrige performance excellence, online education, institutional accreditation, diversity, equity, and inclusion, education technology, active military and veteran support services, and workforce development.

★ ★ ★ ★ ★

THE TERM *LEADERSHIP* REPRESENTS ONE'S ABILITY to guide another toward a desired objective. As an educator and a higher-education administrator, it is my duty to guide my team toward the ultimate objective of ensuring that every one of our students complete his or her desired academic goals. This is accomplished by guiding my team toward a deeper understanding of the mission, values, and strategic goals of our institution. Being mission-driven as a team not only improves our ability to succeed in meeting the tasks and challenges ahead, but it also increases the impact of my leadership. Why? Because it promotes alignment in strategy and practice—thus, empowering the actions of our team to pivot appropriately within the mission and vision. Furthermore, strategically, our operations, actions, and initiatives are mission-driven and data-led, focused on the achievement of our priority objective—student success.

While leadership can be found in theory, it is best learned in practice. Being honest about your interests, strengths, and passions guides the development of one's personal mission statement. Within that mission statement, we find our leadership style. This is essential in providing yourself and the world with your mission- and purpose-driven leadership. Providing leadership through lived experiences, both professional and personal, and other influences of culture, religion, family structure, etc., promotes an authentic leadership approach that is consistent and rooted in the values of who you are. It is that authenticity that assists the leader and their potential/current organization to determine "fit" for each other. Such marriage between the leader and the organization is critical. My authentic approach to leadership was born of my childhood upbringing; I was raised by a single mother who was a K-12 educator. Through her influence, I learned the power of giving of oneself toward the empowerment and development of others. I observed firsthand the hard decisions and sacrifices made by my mother to ensure that I was provided the highest quality of life possible. The years of her love, sacrifice, selfless behavior, and commitment subsequently steered me toward the development of my own leadership traits and characteristics. As I write this chapter, I vividly recall my mother, who for years taught special education, utilizing her own resources and time well beyond her compensated hours, working one-on-one with students and their families to ensure student success. Witnessing this dedication and ultimate investment of herself into her community year after year taught me countless lessons that extend far beyond the pages of leadership theory or the learning outcomes of a leadership seminar.

By no means is this to insinuate that leadership seminars and trainings are not beneficial. They most certainly are, and so are mentorship, instruction, and life lessons. Any development opportunity that exposes learners to theory and provides space for practice of theory is most effective. First, we must learn the canvas and its colors, and then we must be empowered to paint. Just as a medical doctor must practice residency, so should leaders. Through leadership-in-residency, the ability to live out theory and hone critical skills of listening, assessment, discernment, and strategy increases impact and mission advancement.

As you develop your own leadership approach and embrace your leadership-in-residency, there are five characteristics that should serve as your pillars for effective leadership. Those characteristics or five pillars are as follows:

1. **Integrity.** Integrity is the quality of being honest and having strong moral principles or moral uprightness. As an effective leader, integrity is a trait that strategically creates the environment and how your team will interact among themselves and with others. As leaders, you must act with integrity in an effort to convey a standard of honesty and incorruptibility. Devoid of integrity, you compromise the trust others will have in you, which affects your ability to lead and the ability of the team to attain their potential. Integrity is all.

2. **Consistency.** Consistency is the secret weapon that current leaders and future leaders can never underestimate. Consistency is the rhythm of effective leadership. With consistency, there is an implied, tacit understanding of what is expected, how you will be measured, and how you can react. Consistency underscores the value and importance of being fair, rational, and objective with your decisions, assessment, and actions. A lack of consistency results in misdirection and uncertainty, as the team is never quite sure what is coming or how the leader will react. Consequently, they spend unnecessary time looking over their shoulder, wondering

about what will happen versus focusing entirely on what they will do.

3. **Commitment.** Your objective is not achieved simply by being interested in something; it takes a passionate and unyielding belief in what you are about and what you are doing. With this commitment, you have the mindset of a warrior and a strong sense of purpose, and are entirely focused on success and all that it entails. You have the foresight to develop a plan and the discipline to stay the course, knowing that failure is not an option and that you will remain undeterred regardless of the setbacks or obstacles that you encounter.

4. **Ethical Reasoning.** Ethical reasoning, according to Wesleyan University, is the ability to reflect on moral issues in the abstract and in historical narratives within particular traditions. As effective leaders, ethical reasoning represents our ability to guide our team toward the light in any dark situation. Challenges will come, and the complexity of those challenges will vary. Through ethical reasoning, we are able to go beyond the façade of "doing what is right," because depending upon the situation and the variables surrounding a particular situation, "doing what is right" can become clouded with subjectivity.

5. **Inspire and Develop.** An effective leader must possess the ability to inspire and develop others. As the biblical proverb teaches, "As iron sharpens iron, so one person sharpens another." Effective leadership requires leaders to mentally stimulate their team and maintain their fire from within to achieve the task at hand. In

combination with this, an effective leader must have the necessary communication skills in order to convey his or her message and a healthy emotional quotient, which begets a greater understanding of the team and the situation. In addition to guiding the team, the effective leader also builds the team from within. Personnel within your team or span of control who are candidates for increased responsibility should be identified and developed. With proper planning and training, as the team takes on more responsibilities or changes personnel, there is a smooth and continuing operation and transition, including a replacement for yourself, with the cycle continuing.

No one is simply born and earmarked as a leader. Those characteristics and principles are developed over time with key individuals and experiences. I was no exception, and, in addition to my mother, I was blessed with several mentors whose shared experiences shaped my leadership journey. One key person who has served as a professional and personal mentor of mine since 2014 is Dr. Adena Williams Loston, the fourteenth president of the historic St. Philip's College in San Antonio, Texas. Founded in 1898 as a cooking and sewing school for recently emancipated female slaves, St. Philip's College stands as the only institution of higher learning in the nation that carries the dual designation of being a Historical Black College and University (HBCU) and Hispanic Serving Institution (HSI). As a publicly funded two-year community college serving the needs of predominantly Black and Hispanic students, many of whom are from low-income families and educationally underserved, St. Philip's College is one of the five Alamo Community District (ACD) schools located in and serving the greater San Antonio area. Serving as the vice president for student success for St. Philip's College since 2016, I have had the opportunity to serve and learn firsthand from Dr. Loston as she leads this historic institution to achieve historic performance. One of the major lessons I have learned from Dr. Loston over the past several years is how to advance the institutional mission. As effective leaders, we are only as good as our ability to advance the mission at hand. Far too often, good leaders fail to become effective leaders due to poor systems and systems misalignment. Mission advancement requires integrity, consistency, commitment, ethical reasoning, and the ability to inspire and develop others.

Another executive I had the pleasure of learning from was Dr. Ed Welch, who served for 28 years as the president of the University of Charleston in Charleston, West Virginia. Dr. Welch would begin just about every event or meeting with the reciting of the university's mission statement. During my administrative tenure with the University of Charleston, I served as its dean of students and chief student affairs officer. To date, I still have the pleasure of serving this institution in an online-teaching capacity. At the time, I didn't appreciate the power of Dr. Welch having the audience recite the institutional mission, but it set the foundation for what I would ultimately learn from President Loston. It is impossible to advance the institutional mission if you don't know it. This goes back to the characteristic of integrity and the need to walk the talk. As effective leaders, we must walk in the mission in which we serve and cause others to join the journey of mission advancement.

The third mentor I would like to highlight is Dr. Harold Nolte, former district president of Blinn College District in Brenham, Texas. During President Nolte's tenure, I had the pleasure of serving as Director of Student Leadership and Activities and eventually Dean for Student Life. It was Dr. Nolte who taught me the political nature of leadership and the art of winning people. Dr. Nolte made it a point to connect with every student, faculty, staff, or community member he encountered. Honestly, the man knew *everyone*. This taught me that, to be an effective leader, one must possess the ability to connect with and inspire others. Mission advancement is not as simple as delegation; it requires a well-seasoned and intentional approach that begins with a deep understanding of the team you will lead and those vested in the success of your mission.

Effective leaders will be faced with numerous trials and obstacles, and there will also be numerous wins and successes. As a leader, your mettle is tested not so much when things are going well as when they are falling apart. The key to turning trials and tribulations into successes begins with a situational assessment and understanding that you do not stand alone in the mission. Take the time to identify all the factors and implications involved with the opportunity or challenge presented. Seek to approach each opportunity or challenge objectively, and do your absolute best to avoid gut-based decisions (subjectivity). Despite what some may say, your gut may lie to you due to fear or confirmation bias entering the decision-making equation.

Just as importantly, trust your team, and understand that everyone on your team brings with them experience, a set of skills, and the ability to offer insight and various angles to the situation that may not be apparent to you. Understand as well that, despite these efforts, there will be times when defeat will still be experienced. The key here is awareness and having the humility and maturity to accept that not everything turns out the way you planned or hoped it would. It is during these times of adversity and failure when a true leader's effectiveness is displayed, and he or she must rise to the occasion and serve as a focal point for action and inspiration. Above all, honesty, integrity, and transparency with your team throughout the process of initial opportunity, to trial, and even, perhaps, to defeat are what empowers your team to appreciate and learn from the overall experience and further advance their investment in future success.

Throughout my leadership career, I have learned that there is no one-size-fits-all, as each individual and each situation is different. Thus, you cannot be so rigid or committed to one style or approach that you hazard success. However, most people, like myself, have primary modes of operation when it comes to leadership, and, here, I am no exception. With respect to my personal leadership style(s), I consider myself a hybrid of servant leader and transformational leader, and there are reasons for that. The hybrid component is a direct reflection of my personal mission statement and my upbringing, which guides my personal actions with myself, my family, and the community I serve—"Mordecai Ian Brownlee empowers people and builds systems that empower people."

Some of the best advice I ever received from my mother was to manage my life like a business, and every business requires a mission statement. I certainly would encourage you to develop a mission statement for yourself if you have not already and review your actions daily to ensure mission alignment. If you don't submit it to writing, the chances of it coming to fruition are compromised. Doing this will help you focus on what you are about, what you need to do, and what you need to change, as leadership is a continuum. It will make you not only a more effective leader, but it will also make you an all-around more effective person, ensuring you maintain a healthy balance between your professional career and your personal life. In addition, I would encourage you to seek out mentorship and advice from those who, after careful observation, align with your mission. It is important to remember that your mentors are people, too, which means they are flawed. However, their wisdom and advice reflect the lived experiences which have shaped their perspective—wisdom that will prove beneficial on your journey. It is also important to be intentional with whom you align yourself and from whom you gather your knowledge and wisdom. To exercise the metaphor of water representing knowledge, tainted water can spread and foul the purest of springs.

While nothing can serve as a substitute for having mentors and living and learning the experience of leadership, there are some options for augmenting your expertise as a means to fine-tune or improve. The leadership-training field is rife with courses, seminars, and buzzwords, and exposure to these options presents opportunities to learn. However, despite good intentions, not all leadership training is created equal, and, in many instances, it is ineffective. In this regard, it is important to look at the various methodologies and approaches available and to determine what the desired outcome is. The return on investment depends on the desired outcome, which is a direct reflection of the quality of the pre-work completed when scouring potential leadership-training opportunities. A further complicating factor is the new environment and economy we are faced with, which will continue post-COVID-19, where adjustments have to be made to how training was formerly conducted. This yields a further impediment to the ability to conduct effective leadership training, and how this pans out remains to be seen. Personally, I have found that pursuing leadership-training opportunities that are organized and led by fellow educators provides me with a deep sense of content alignment, situational relevancy, and applied-knowledge sharing, which, importantly, can continue after the session and serve as a means of reinforcement. Planning (which is the pre-work), a quality curriculum, and quality instructors all lend themselves to a quality leadership-training experience.

In hindsight, I have no regrets with my leadership journey. There is one thing I am certain I did right from the onset, which to me is one of the most important traits necessary to become an effective leader, and that is to focus on accountability. And here, it does start with you. Leaders must embrace the responsibility of holding themselves accountable—first and foremost. Holding yourself accountable and ensuring you have alignment with your principles and values and those of the organization will be an ongoing manifestation of your personal and professional integrity, and serve as an example for others.

I sincerely hope my story and insights have provided you with some ideas and inspiration for your leadership journey and your personal life. In your journey, whatever you do and however you do it, always seize the opportunity on ways in which you can grow by trying new things. The world is ever changing, innovation is essential, and you must continually adapt in order to succeed and meet your fullest potential. God bless you, your family, and your endeavors.

CHAPTER THIRTEEN

JACKIE FREEDMAN

★ ★ ★ ★ ★

Jackie Freedman's fascination with great leadership started early. In her first full-time position, as Assistant Director of Catering at a Sheraton Hotel, she was responsible for a staff of more than 125 and saw firsthand how leadership's attitudes affected people's performance and corporate results. Today, as the founder of Delta-V Strategies, she has spent more than 20 years working with leaders and their teams, equipping them with the knowledge and insights they need to navigate organizational growth. In her capacity as a consultant, facilitator, and coach, she has guided clients in strategic planning and supported their implementation efforts. She has created and delivered professional-development sessions to thousands of people on a wide variety of leadership-development topics. Prior to her work at Delta-V Strategies, Jackie was the National Marketing Manager at Red Devil, Inc., an international consumer-products company, where she was responsible for more than 1,000 products. While there, she introduced a new concept in merchandising and was named one of the "40 Who Are Lighting Up the Point-of-Purchase World" by P-O-P Times. She led efforts to launch an entirely new product category and restructured the process for handling customer issues. Jackie served as president of the Rutgers Business School Alumni Association, leading the 70-person board through a massive restructuring—a structure that remains in place today. She is the author of Updraft: The Aerodynamics of Great Leadership *and is a sought-after speaker on the connection between leadership and organizational performance. She has been a guest on radio stations across the country and on podcasts internationally.*

★ ★ ★ ★ ★

LEAD. LEADER. LEADERSHIP.

ALL THREE SHARE THE SAME ROOT WORD. But while most of us can fairly easily define "lead" or "leader," it gets much more complex when we try to tackle the word "leadership." The simplicity of the verb "to lead" sits in sharp contrast to the complexity of talents, behaviors, attitudes, skills, etc., required by true leadership. Young children play "follow the leader," where one child is designated the leader and gets to choose the group's next activity (e.g., clapping, jumping, singing). But right away, this brings up an important question: Just because someone is *in* a leadership position, does that make them a leader? And if we continue with this line of questioning, even if it does technically make them a leader, does it mean they are providing leadership?

When I ask a group of people, "How many of you have worked for a great leader?" I'll see some hands go up. Then I clarify. "I'm not talking about a good manager." Some hands go down. "I'm not talking about a good person to work for. We're talking great leadership." Most hands, if not all, go down. Like the endangered Northern Spotted Owl, great leaders are far too rare.

I consider myself extremely lucky. I had the privilege of working for someone I consider a great leader. It was early in my career—in fact, it was my first job out of college—and in an industry I didn't intend to enter. But when I interviewed with Lisa for the Assistant Director of Catering at a Sheraton Hotel, I could see this was going to be special. As she downed four or five espressos during the course of our meeting, she explained that we had a unionized staff of about 125 people, oversaw up to 20 events in a day, including 300-person weddings, and covered for the sales department over the weekends. It wasn't what I was looking for, but, in an interesting twist to the typical interview, Lisa shared with me her plans and vision for the department and told me why she felt I would be successful in the role. It was the proverbial offer I couldn't refuse.

Fortunately, my instincts were right. I acquired tremendous experience managing an extremely diverse group of people and dealt with some extraordinary situations—the wrongful arrest of an employee, the threats of an angry fired employee, and the behavior of some drunken clients, to name just a few. I'd like to say that Lisa was a powerful mentor to me, but that wouldn't really be true. In order to ensure coverage for all the department's events, which typically started before 7 a.m. and often ran until well after midnight, Lisa and I worked different shifts. So, it didn't take long before I was on my own, often jumping from the frying pan straight into the fire.

But it worked. Though we didn't spend a lot of time on the operational aspects of running events, Lisa made sure I knew the truly important things. Right off the bat, she shared with me her vision and goals for the department—how she wanted to expand sales and offerings, how we'd need to increase staff and identify people who could move into supervisory positions, and some preliminary thoughts on the kinds of staff training we would need. She was crystal clear about her expectations and about what behaviors were and weren't tolerated. She treated people fairly and respectfully but set the bar high and held people accountable—and expected that I would do the same. She introduced me to the staff, saying that she and I were "interchangeable"—she expected them to treat me and work with me the same way they did her, and she took the opportunity to remind everybody of what we were there to accomplish and how we were expected to accomplish it. Even when she wasn't in the building, Lisa's influence was palpable, and the staff's response was amazing.

What fuels my passion and drives me to do the work I do is that I saw with my own eyes and experienced firsthand the power of great leadership. We had a large staff that hailed from Newark, New Jersey, and the surrounding area. Most of them took buses or walked to work, and yet they were rarely late and called if they had an issue. Despite the union environment, everyone went over and above, pitching in even when it "wasn't their job." They brought us suggestions for improving processes so we could turn rooms over faster, which enabled us to support more events. Our group of wait staff and housemen (the guys who set up tables, chairs, etc.) surpassed departmental sales goals and garnered stellar customer-service metrics.

And yet, much of what I learned from Lisa wasn't even obvious at the time. In fact, I can't discount the impact of the bad leaders with whom I've worked. It would make a very strange *Thank You* note, but, in many ways, I'm indebted to them for the opportunity to see how destructive their behavior was and how it undermined the very goals they were trying to achieve. Comparing and contrasting these later experiences with those from early on enabled me to pinpoint the factors that contributed so tremendously to Lisa's success. This combination of experiences shaped my approach and philosophy by highlighting the power of leadership and by illustrating, in great detail, what happens in its absence.

THE IMPACT OF GREAT LEADERSHIP

The experience of working with Lisa was nothing less than life changing. She laid out her vision for the department, explained and modeled the behaviors she expected, and then brought me to the edge of the precipice and . . . . pushed. But she armed me with the confidence that I could do what was needed, both with clients and our team. It was an incredibly fast-paced environment, and I had tremendous freedom to act and to make decisions—knowing she would always have my back. All these years later, I look back on that experience and can't even begin to assess how my time with Lisa impacted my career and my life—I wouldn't be who I am or where I am today without her.

When I talk to others who've had the rare opportunity of working with a great leader, I hear similar themes of people successfully tackling things they didn't think they could do, learning to leverage their strengths, expanding their abilities, and gaining the confidence and the desire to go looking for new challenges. Like that one teacher you still remember who didn't give up on you and got you through algebra or biology or whatever subject was kicking your butt, great leaders leave a lasting impression. They inspire and elevate those around them, helping all of us achieve more than we knew we could—and all the while moving the organization toward its goals and objectives.

Interestingly enough, when I speak to those designated "great leaders" and ask about what they are most proud of, they talk about *people*. Yes, under their leadership, their organizations have achieved remarkable results and done great things, however, it's the people they developed and the impact they had on them that you'll hear about. They fondly recount stories of people they still hear from, often finding out years later that their impact was far beyond anything they had imagined. It's a lot like listening to a proud parent. And even if you ask about the accomplishments attributed to them and their leadership, they'll tell you how their team worked long hours to make it happen or how their people overcame a major obstacle.

Of course, there are many whose teams or organizations boast impressive achievements but who have gotten those results in a way that left people feeling demeaned and diminished. I've worked with many CEOs and executives who get results by telling people what to do and how to do it, using their positions to demand compliance. They tend to be rather critical and rarely acknowledge the contributions of others, focusing strictly on their own results. Their employees call them many things but not "great leaders." True leadership encompasses not just the successes and achievements of the leader and their organization but also the impact they've had on those around them. It's not just about getting things done.

LEADERSHIP PHILOSOPHY

To me, leadership is the ability to supercharge people, developing their talents and harnessing their efforts in a way that supports the growth of the organization. To do this, great leaders need to focus their attention in three main areas: ensuring the organization has what it needs, setting and articulating the direction, and nurturing and protecting the culture. While all three areas are crucial, the last one is undoubtedly the most challenging and time-consuming. It cannot be ignored. It cannot be neglected. It cannot be delegated. And it goes right to the heart of great leadership. Nowhere is the leader's impact on those around them, both individually and collectively, more apparent than in the culture of the organization. Lisa created and maintained an energizing and inclusive culture. It was characterized by the highest levels of respect for all people, very high standards, and a touch of formality. It permeated every aspect of what we did.

The culture you create is a direct reflection of who you are and what you believe and has everything to do with the impact you have on others. Generally speaking, do you see leadership as a fulfilling journey and enjoy nurturing and developing those around you . . . or do you see people as a necessary evil? Do you believe that people want to do a good job . . . or do you think they want to do as little as possible and just collect their paychecks? Do you trust people to do what's best for the organization . . . or do you believe they'd rob you blind if they got the opportunity?

It is these underlying beliefs and attitudes that come together to make up what I refer to as your *leadership philosophy*. To me, this is your overall approach to the discipline of leadership. Your answers to these questions are foundational to your leadership philosophy and reflect your attitudes, beliefs, and experiences. Every interaction, every discussion, and every decision broadcasts your deepest convictions, giving rise to your organization's culture. Where many leaders go wrong is when they think that people don't see through the inconsistencies between what their leaders say and what they do; leaders can easily underestimate the damage this does to their authenticity and integrity. In one company, the leaders talked about how important people were (certainly a common platitude), and, yet, the leadership team was late to almost every meeting and then spent much of it focused on their phones and tablets. Do you think people felt important? The actions of the leadership team negated their words. People didn't feel valued, and the culture reflected the truth of leadership's philosophy, which included an inflated sense of the leadership team's importance over that of everyone else. Never lose sight of the fact that, as a leader, you have to walk the talk and hold yourself to a higher standard. The impact you have on those around you will determine whether they simply do their jobs or rise to any occasion.

THE KEY TO BEING A GREAT LEADER

So, if great leadership goes beyond getting things done and depends on the kind of impact you have on those around you, then what's the key to success? I can tell you in one word (okay, two words, but they're hyphenated): self-awareness. If the impact you have on others is crucial to your success as a leader, then the trick is to be intentional about the impact and the effect you are having. While it sounds simple enough, it is far from easy. Most of us are moving quickly and operating unconsciously—essentially on autopilot. Observing, studying, and evaluating your own behavior take concentration, effort, and an openness that few possess.

While most of the leaders I've worked with are quick to say they are very self-aware, few actually are. Not only do they not see how they are impacting people, but they are quick to defend their actions rather than consider possible alternatives. Great leaders understand the difference between having a big ego and having healthy self-esteem. A strong ego is an inflated self-image, often existing to mask insecurities. A strong sense of self, on the other hand, allows people to see and accept themselves as they are, with a more realistic picture of their strengths and weaknesses. Recognizing and accepting weaknesses open the door to learning and development.

Self-awareness means looking inward to understand your values, motivations, feelings, reactions, strengths, weaknesses, and so on. Self-awareness also means looking outward to understand the gap between what you see and how others truly perceive you. Going it alone can be difficult. Blind spots, by their very nature, are hard to detect. Today, there is a plethora of courses, assessments, and coaches available to help on this journey. Start by learning more about your communication style and your level of emotional intelligence (often referred to as *emotional quotient*). Assess your integrity—do you do what you say you will, even on the most casual commitments (e.g., "I'll get back to you on that.")? Force yourself to see things from a different perspective. For instance, when reviewing an interaction, I often ask myself, "What was my goal, and did I achieve it?" along with "What could I have done differently, and how would that have impacted the outcome?" Get useful feedback by finding what Tasha Eurich calls "loving critics"—people who are invested in your success and are able and willing to tell you the truth.

Self-awareness will also help you identify where and when your natural tendencies could hamper your effectiveness as a leader, while simultaneously guiding your development efforts. For instance, no matter how wonderful your team, there will come a time when you will need to address a problematic performance issue. Avoiding these kinds of interactions will jeopardize your effectiveness as a leader and undermine the culture you've built. Recognizing that it's a weak point, you could build your skills in related areas like difficult conversations, active listening, and fostering accountability. The most successful leaders cultivate an ever-expanding toolkit of techniques and competencies that allows them to tailor their approach to whatever is appropriate to the moment, the person, the situation, and so on. The more tools and techniques you can choose from, the more likely you are to have the impact—and get the results—you want. Leadership requires an ever-expanding list of both strategic and tactical skills—the kind that can take a lifetime to master; great leaders are never done with their own development efforts.

START TODAY

All this talk about learning and development would seem to suggest that great leaders can be made, and I believe that's true. I've watched people embrace and assimilate the concepts we've discussed and begin adjusting their behavior to close the gap between who they are and who they want to be. But having said that, the most successful had a growth mindset, were not just *open* to coaching but *eager* to get it, were not afraid to ask for help, were willing to accept feedback, and were grateful for the opportunity. These people were truly excited to be moving into positions where they could help others develop and grow.

The other good news is that, if you want to move into leadership, you don't need a leadership position in order to start developing and honing your skills. Since so much of leadership springs from your impact on others, you can begin right now. Think about the characteristics you'd like to embody and how you want people to experience you—as a leader *and* as a person. Observe your interactions, noticing what you did and how you acted when you felt you were modeling the desired traits. When you fall short, an important part of the process is to think about what made you react the way you did and what you could have done differently. While great leadership is among the most challenging of jobs, it is also one of the most gratifying and fulfilling. I invite you to take on this challenge—the world is in need of great leaders, and you could be one of them.

CHAPTER FOURTEEN

JON S. RENNIE

★ ★ ★ ★ ★

Leadership Is a People Business

Jon is the Co-Founder, President, and CEO of Peak Demand Inc., a premier manufacturer of components for electrical utilities. He is a former U.S. Navy Nuclear Submarine Officer who made seven deployments during the Cold War. Before starting Peak Demand, he worked 22 years as vice president for three global companies. He led eight different manufacturing businesses that generated more than $250M in annual sales. He is the author of the best-selling leadership book I Have the Watch: Becoming a Leader Worth Following, *and a new book titled* All in the Same Boat: Lead Your Organization Like a Nuclear Submariner. *He hosts the popular Deep Leadership podcast, where he interviews leaders and entrepreneurs to share their insights and experiences. He has more than 30 years of military and business-leadership experience. The most important lesson he's learned during these years is that leadership matters. He knows*

that strong leadership can make a significant difference
in the performance of any organization. He shares his
thoughts and insights on business and leadership with
a singular mission: to build a world with better bosses.

★ ★ ★ ★ ★

AFTER A LONG FLIGHT AND AN UNCOMFORTABLE RIDE in the back of an old cab from Jacksonville, Florida, to Kings Bay, Georgia, I finally arrived. I had orders to report to the USS *Tennessee*, an Ohio-class ballistic-missile nuclear submarine. I was a 23-year-old ensign, the lowest ranking officer in the U.S. Navy. Fresh out of submarine school, I was young and inexperienced, but, according to the Navy, I was ready for the fleet.

With my seabag over my shoulder, I entered the cavernous covered dry-dock area. I saw the *Tennessee* for the first time. The 560-foot warship looked massive, and everywhere around her was activity. I stood for a few moments and took in the sights, sounds, and smells. Hundreds of sailors and shipyard workers worked feverishly on this marvel of engineering to prepare her to go to sea.

I had spent four years studying engineering, a year in nuclear-power training, and three months in submarine school. I was about to fulfill a childhood dream. I was entering into the fast-paced, technical, and dangerous world of underwater warfare in a Cold War that had lasted more than four decades. As I considered the challenge that stood before me, I suddenly realized I wasn't ready for this.

The truth is, when it comes to leadership, none of us are ever really ready for it. Even if you are born with the natural skills to be a great leader, you need practice. You can read books and understand the theory, but ultimately you need to *be a leader* to truly understand leadership. As a young officer on my first deployment, I felt like I was in over my head. I was assigned to lead the reactor-controls division on the *Tennessee*, the small team who operated and maintained the nuclear-reactor instrumentation. The chief petty officer, my right-hand man, had almost as many years in the Navy as I had been alive. Every sailor in the division was highly skilled and had years of experience. When I looked around, I realized I was the least-qualified person on the team, yet I was the leader.

Back then, I thought that leaders had to have all the answers. Being the least knowledgeable person on the team felt intimidating. Now, after more than thirty years of leading men and women in the military, Corporate America, and my own manufacturing company, I realize that that thinking is wrong. With all the experience I have today, I still don't know everything, but I've discovered something even more important: I've learned that all the answers I need to lead effectively are in the minds of my team. The collective wisdom of employees is always greater than the ideas of one manager. Great leaders don't need to have all the answers, but they need to have the right questions. They don't need to know everything, but they need to know how to get the most from their team members.

Leading people can be difficult, which is why there have been more than 15,000 books written on leadership. Each one has added to our collective understanding of this complex subject. Yet, with all this knowledge, our practice remains subpar at best. According to the latest Gallup survey, close to 70% of employees remain disengaged at work. The primary reason for low employee engagement is poor leadership. At least in the business world, we are not applying what we have learned. In a way, the so-called "experts" have made leadership more complicated than it needs to be. In my experience, it's always better to keep things simple. Leadership is like anything else. When we reduce it to its essential components, we can gain a better understanding. For me, I like the definition written by *New York Times* bestseller author and business leader, Kevin Kruse. Kevin says, "Leadership is a process of social influence, which maximizes the efforts of [people] toward the achievement of a goal." This definition best describes the three most essential leadership elements—people, influence, and a goal. I've learned that, if you get these right, you'll be an effective leader.

I served for four years on the *USS Tennessee* and spent almost two years of my life underwater. I made seven strategic-deterrent patrols and witnessed the end of the Cold War firsthand. I successfully led hundreds of sailors and learned a lot about myself in the process. It was the most important education I've ever received. During those formative years, the leadership lessons I learned provided a strong foundation for the rest of my career. As it turns out, a submerged submarine at sea is a remarkable place to observe organizational behavior and leadership in action. It was also the perfect environment for practicing leadership.

If you think about it, life on a submarine is genuinely unique. It's almost like going to work and one day having your boss lock the doors and tell you that no one can leave for the next ninety days. You are stuck with the people you deploy with. There is no escape and no time off. You perform difficult and often dangerous work with a group of strangers from every part of the country, every race, and every background. To top it off, it's all done under the ocean, in close quarters, far away from friends and family.

One of the most powerful lessons I learned in those early years as a young officer in the Navy was that leadership is a people business. In the tight confines of the USS *Tennessee*, I learned a lot about the people I worked with. We stood watch together for hours on end. I knew everything about them, and they knew everything about me. There was a tight bond. We were a brotherhood and had each others' backs. The truth is, we were all in the same boat. Whether it was the Soviets or thousands of pounds of crushing seawater above us, the enemy was always outside the pressure hull, waiting for us to make a mistake. The people inside the hull were our only hope for survival.

What was distinctive about the submarine force compared to other military branches is that there was no room for special privileges. Officers and senior enlisted sailors were treated just like the rest of the crew. We ate the same foods, wore the same uniform, and slept in the same coffin-sized racks. When we were low on freshwater, no one showered. When the galley was shut down, we all ate cold cuts. When we ran drills, everyone donned an emergency air-breathing mask and "sucked rubber." Every member of the crew was critical to our success, and no one got special treatment. We worked together, celebrated together, and suffered together.

Every member of the crew was necessary; we just had different roles to play. We all had a job to do, from the lowest seaman pulling crank duty on the mess decks to the commanding officer writing the night orders. We were all essential to the safe and effective operation of the *Tennessee*. We were in it together. Every person played a critical role in carrying out our mission. This concept has always stuck with me and helped me appreciate every employee's importance, regardless of rank or experience. I also learned that, when you demonstrate this behavior as a leader, you can quickly create a culture of mutual respect throughout a team.

The first chance to apply everything I had learned on the *Tennessee* on a large scale came five years after I got out of the Navy. I had worked in various department management positions at a multinational engineering company when I got the call. My actions had caught the attention of upper management, and they promoted me to plant manager. At just 32 years old, I moved my family to South Carolina to become the general manager of an underperforming manufacturing plant with 160 employees. I would be the youngest general manager ever to lead this operation. When I first drove into the parking lot and considered the challenge that stood before me, I knew I still had a lot to learn—but I was excited to put my experience into practice.

The first thing I did was focus on the people. I spent a significant amount of time in the plant to get to know the employees who worked in the business. I spent my days on the shop floor, walking around and talking to people. Like I did on the *Tennessee*, I got to know the employees, and they got to know me. I learned their names, where they came from, how long they'd worked in the company, and what they did in their spare time. I found the workforce to be intelligent, hardworking, and curious about me and the business's future. I discovered that they each cared deeply about the plant's success.

I also met with the entire leadership team and got to know them as well. I had individual meetings with each of them and asked three questions: What's going well? What needs to be fixed? And, if you were in my shoes, what would be the first thing you would do? I was surprised that most of the ideas in these meetings coalesced around a few key topics. By getting to know them and talking through these issues, I began to understand what needed to get done.

The one interesting thing I observed as I got to know the employees is that many didn't know much about the final products we produced. When I asked the employees what they did, they would tell me about the machine they operated or the parts they assembled. When I dug a little deeper and asked more details, most employees couldn't explain how their efforts affected the final product that we produced. There was a disconnect between the work they were doing and its significance to the business.

On the *Tennessee*, by contrast, it was apparent how your job affected the mission. As a helmsman, you knew that if you failed to steer the boat correctly, the boat could run aground. The employees at this plant didn't have that direct connection, and I needed to address this. When it comes to motivating people, it's important to connect their work to the company's mission. They need to understand how their actions affect the performance of the business. Every person, regardless of position, wants to do worthwhile work and know their efforts matter. So, as a leadership team, we set about teaching our employees why their work made a difference.

We began by simply teaching them what the company did. The factory produced circuit breakers for the electrical-power industry, so we explained how important these products were for keeping the lights on. We reviewed this with employees every day and in every meeting. We showed them how the work they were doing kept the power flowing to hospitals, schools, and their own homes. Instead of just making parts or building a widget, they began to see their work as meaningful. They began to understand that every employee was essential to building a high-quality circuit breaker that could keep the power flowing. The employees' attitudes toward their jobs changed almost overnight. They realized they were doing something important, something that mattered.

We also developed and communicated goals throughout the plant. The company had overall financial goals, but we needed to create targets that mattered to each operator. We needed to set goals for quality, cost, delivery, safety—things the employees could control. Once these were developed, we communicated these goals in daily stand-up meetings on the shop floor. Every day, we reviewed our performance to the goals and discussed corrective actions if needed. Measuring our progress became a regular routine in the business. We also had monthly all-employee meetings, in which we would review the full-plant results. Communicating goals and measuring performance became part of the culture.

As a result of all the work that we did, the plant continued to improve. Within six months, our performance began to exceed our targets consistently. In just eighteen months, we became the best-performing manufacturing plant in our division. We set new records for orders, revenues, and profits, but more importantly, we began feeling like a team. Employees sensed they were part of something special. As upper management took notice of our efforts, they recognized us with various accolades and awards. They also decided to transfer more product lines to our plant because of our reputation. As a result, the business continued to grow. In my third year leading the plant, we were nominated for the manufacturer-of-the-year award for the state of South Carolina. Although we finished second in the competition, there was a sense of pride throughout the plant for being selected.

Former U.S. Navy SEAL Jocko Willink says, "Leadership is the single greatest factor in any team's performance. Whether a team succeeds or fails is all up to the leader." What I did to improve this plant wasn't rocket science. It was a common-sense approach based on the proven lessons I'd learned in the Navy. On the *Tennessee*, I learned that people matter and that leadership is a people business. That's why I spent so much time with employees to build a solid relationship with them. I also showed them how important the work they were doing was and how every employee was critical to our success. I focused on establishing clear goals that each employee could control. I set expectations, measured performance, and followed through relentlessly. These simple techniques made this manufacturing operation a top performer, and they can work in your organization as well.

The problem with most managers today is that they are promoted not because of their leadership skills but because they were a strong individual contributor. Many of these managers slip back into what they are comfortable with: being a doer and not a leader. Instead of doing the work of leadership, they spend their days in meetings, writing emails, and on conference calls. They never apply the three most essential elements of leadership—people, influence, and goals. They fail to build a relationship with their teams, establish clear goals, and motivate employees to accomplish them. The failure of the leader results in poor performance, disengaged employees, and high turnover.

When it comes to leadership, none of us are ever really ready for it. But the good news is that you don't have to have all the answers. To be an effective leader, you only need to tap into your team's collective wisdom and motivate them toward a goal. The best leaders know that every employee plays a critical role in carrying out the mission. The leader's job is to make sure everyone knows their role and how their actions affect the overall performance. In the end, it doesn't have to be complicated, as long as you remember that leadership is a people business.

CHAPTER FIFTEEN

ALAN LERCHBACKER

★ ★ ★ ★ ★

Alan Lerchbacker spent 26 years in the U.S. Navy as an Engineering Duty Officer and Navy Diver. He ran operations for the 2,500-person shipyard in Guam. He then went to Long Beach Naval Shipyard and was key to making the BRAC process one the Department of Labor used as an example. He and his team placed more than 2,700 people in less than 11 months. Alan was the first CEO for Austal USA, an Australian Company. He teamed with General Dynamics and Boeing to win a $4 billion contract for Littoral Combat Ship, LCS. Alan grew Austal USA from 66 to more than 1200 employees, and, today, Austal has more than 5,000 employees. As President of Taylor-Dunn, Alan grew this 50-year-old company into a GSA government provider, expanded sales to more than 40 countries, and also helped steer the company to become a division of $9 billion Polaris. Most recently, Alan acquired Naval Coating, Inc., a 50-year-old company, and was their CEO for 4 years. He grew this company from 44 to more than 200 employees. Today, Mr. Lerchbacker serves *on several boards, including the San Diego Armed Forces YMCA and the Board of Trustees for the United States Naval Academy. Alan has an Executive MBA from the Peter Drucker School of Business and also a Master's in Mechanical Engineering from the Naval Post Graduate School, Monterey, California.*

★ ★ ★ ★ ★

WHILE SOME OF YOU HAVE SEEN the movie *Chariots of Fire*, I have lived it. When I was ten, my Mom took me to the Elyria Library. I found a book almost immediately, and this book would change my life. The book was *Flying Spikes*, by Jackson Scholtz and was *Chariots of Fire* from an American point of view. I was so inspired that, when I arrived home, I informed my mother and father that I was going to be in the Olympics, which is *not* something you want to tell very German and Scot parents. The next morning, my Mom woke me up at 0530, told me it was time to go running, and pointed to the door! It was winter in Ohio, and it was freezing and snowing. However, if I was going to be in the Olympics and be a runner, my mom knew was I was going to have to *run*. So, off I went that morning and every morning thereafter. That was one of my first examples of effective leadership—hard, straightforward, no nonsense, a true commitment with a shared vision, and action to make it happen. Looking back, I was so blessed to have parents who never quit, never knew the meaning of a down day or a tough time, and imbued me with the values that enabled me to be committed and fulfilled every day of my life.

Two years later, just to show you how Midwest we were, my Dad declared we were going camping in Washington, DC, and would tour the Capitol. Two days later, off we went. Five hours later we were somewhere off Interstate 50 just outside of DC, pulling into a KOA (Kampground of America). We set up camp, and I departed for my daily run. During my run, to my surprise and excitement, I saw a sign: "Five miles to Annapolis." This is significant for two reasons. First, because both my Mom and Dad were enlisted in the Navy, and every year, we would watch *Victory at Sea* following our annual viewing of the Army-Navy game; secondly, I was in the midst of a career change. Now you might wonder why someone my age would be having a career change so early on, and the answer is pretty straightforward and representative of the times and the environment. If you are from Ohio, specifically Cleveland, there are three things you can do. One, you can become a priest. Two, you could work for U.S. Steel, as did all seven of my Dad's brothers and his four brothers-in-law. Three, you could join the Navy. During my formative years, all the way up through eighth grade, it was a given that I was destined for option one, the priesthood. However, during my time in the eighth grade, I went through a transformation. Up until that point, I had avoided girls like the plague and didn't want anything to do with them. Somehow, for reasons not entirely clear to me at the time, my outlook changed considerably; I discovered girls were actually pretty special. With the priesthood now a non-starter and having never had a desire to work for U.S. Steel, option three was now the intended career path.

So, to me, seeing the sign for Annapolis was a favorable omen. Upon my return, I informed my parents I had seen a sign to where the guys in the Army-Navy game go to school and that I wanted to see Annapolis. Upon hearing this, my parents pivoted on a dime, and instead of going to DC, we drove to Annapolis. We had the tour of a lifetime! Reflecting on the tour during the ride back to Ohio, I informed my parents I was going to this school. My Dad, even though he lacked a formal education due to work commitments at an early age, was one of the smartest persons I ever met. And as usual, he didn't miss a beat and responded that I'd better get to know a congressman. He said nothing more after that, but he knew my makeup and how I responded to challenges. I nodded, indicating I understood, which was the genesis of my plan to gain admittance to Annapolis. My plan was three-fold—academic, athletic, and get to know a congressman. I kept my grades up and continued to run through high school. I was very competitive in the sport, winning races in several meets, both locally and beyond, which garnered some attention from some colleges, although there was only one on my radar. With persistence being its own reward, I eventually established a relationship with the congressman. I applied to the Naval Academy, and, with a congressional endorsement, I was admitted. The day I received my notice was exhilarating and not without some relief as I had only Plan A—Annapolis.

After I graduated from high school, that summer my Mom and Dad drove me to the Naval Academy, where each one of the 1409 soon-to-be-Plebes was personally greeted along with their parents by the Superintendent, Admiral James Calvert. Admiral Calvert cut an impressive figure, to say the least, and was an accomplished individual, with one of his notable accomplishments being the Commanding Officer of the first submarine to crack through the ice at the North Pole. He was articulate and straightforward, a style I admired. I recall him stating, "Four years from now, when some of you go to graduate, more than one-third of you will *not* be there." When I heard Admiral Calvert's statement, I vowed to myself to see this through and do whatever it would take to graduate. My Dad also gave me further motivation in his usual, direct, no-nonsense manner by telling me that, if I came home, it had better be in a box. As Admiral Calvert predicted, we lost more than 500 before we graduated, and nearly 300 in that first year, but I did graduate and was proudly commissioned an officer in the United States Navy, thus fulfilling option three of my career path.

Without a doubt, the values and lessons learned during my time at the Naval Academy were of incalculable value in both the military and civilian sector. However, none of this would have been possible without what I see as the first three ingredients required for someone to be successful. The first is finding something you believe in and having that goal; the second is to have the discipline and tenacity to act on it; the third is the need to persevere and be resilient and able to withstand the obstacles and roadblocks that you encounter. Notwithstanding these ingredients, my growth and success were also made possible by another factor which everyone not only *needs* but *must have* to succeed—a mentor, or, more precisely, mentors. Early on, likely due to the respect I had for my parents and how I followed their advice, I was continually seeking advice from others as a way not only to learn but to either reinforce that I was doing the right thing and headed in the right direction or make a course adjustment if it was necessary. I have never had a problem doing this; I consider my willingness and openness to the opinions, even criticism, of others to be a strength. Over the course of my career, I have been blessed to have a number of mentors, as well as several people who were a source of inspiration.

One person who had a profound influence on me was Admiral Jerry Tuttle. He was "Captain Tuttle" back then, but all 5'2" of him was packed with more energy than anyone else I have ever met. I met Captain Tuttle while I was standing the EOOW watch on the aircraft carrier *USS John F. Kennedy* (CVA-67). The first time was when he came into Central, nine stories down inside the depths of the ship, at 0325 hours. I announced, "Attention on Deck," having no idea who this very senior officer was invading my watch station. I asked if he would like to sit in my seat, but he said he would rather stand and watch. I then went on dutifully, trying to appear confident, while grimacing inside the entire time, wondering what this officer wanted and what fate was lying in store for me due to his presence. After about an hour of him looking around the space, he told me he wanted me to teach him how to stand watch. He said since he was going to be our new Commanding Officer, he wanted to get to know as much about the men and ship as possible. To say I was surprised is an understatement, and I tried to hide my amazement. I responded, "Yes, sir," and, over the next several hours, we went through a stunning role reversal. I was the teacher, and he was the student. During the entire time, he listened, followed my instructions, and did quite well, as he was quick on the uptake. You could see he was genuinely interested and appreciative of my time. As the watch ended, he asked to be relieved (like I had a choice), thanked me for my time, and headed topside. Not long after that, he assumed Command,

and after the Change of Command Ceremony in Norfolk on Monday, on Tuesday morning an announcement was made on the ship's 1MC, which is the ship's announcing system, that "the ship is underway." Now we all knew this was not possible since we were still at Pier 12 in Norfolk, Virginia, and we were further surprised to see that Captain Tuttle had pulled the brow up. As it turns out, there was a method to his perceived madness, and it was genius and inspiring.

When Captain Tuttle came onboard, we had just failed inspection, had more than 300 sailors UA (unauthorized absence), a reenlistment rate below 50%, and 900 mast cases pending. When I say "mast," I refer to "Captain's Mast," which is a term for a military hearing for a crew member. Oftentimes the XO, or Executive Officer, will handle the cases on behalf of the Captain, but not in this instance. Captain Tuttle stated no one was going ashore until *all* 900 mast cases had been heard and that he would hear every one of them. For the next 30 hours, with hardly a break, he listened to every case, of which 30 were in my division. He was fair and even-handed, and he exhibited genuine concern for each crew member's situation. In that first 30 hours, he changed the culture of our ship simply by showing that he cared, listening to people, and knowing how to take care of those young men who could be good leaders someday but who had made a mistake. Another thing he did was to interview every crew member who was within six months of their EOS, or Expiration of Service. He sat with every crew member, listened to them, made suggestions, and asked what he could do to help. I could go on and on about the things he did, but the results were staggering. We passed our next inspection with flying colors, the list of UAs virtually disappeared, and our reenlistment rate was more than 95% in less than a year.

Shifting back to the topic of the importance of mentors, I try to follow Christ's example. He had twelve apostles, and everywhere I go and every leadership opportunity I have had, I have striven to find twelve mentors to work with me. My first two mentors in the Navy were Captain Walt Marquardt and his wife, Shirley. For whatever reason, they took a liking to me, exhibiting genuine concern for my person and well-being. They literally adopted me as a midshipman. I studied down in their basement almost every night, and Walt is the reason I have pursued an engineering profession. Anytime I had a problem I wanted to discuss, was feeling discouraged, or even was a bit rudderless, Walt and Shirley were always there to provide support and guidance and enable me to stay even-keeled. They were instrumental in helping me not only survive but flourish at the Naval Academy. And even after graduation, they were a continuing guiding light and took many phone calls from me, regardless of the time. To this day, I am humbled by their love and support.

Captain "Black Bart" Bartholomew was another mentor of mine. "Black Bart" as he was known, was in charge of all diving and salvage for the U.S. Navy. I knew him, although casually, which is the way many mentor arrangements start out, but soon, that was to change. On January 28, 1986, Admiral David Robinson, another one of my mentors, called me into his office. I had been working out, playing basketball at the gym, when I was informed by an aide that the Admiral needed to see me immediately. I quickly cleaned up, changed into my uniform, and was in his office within thirty minutes. Admiral Robinson cut to the chase. He stated the Space Shuttle *Challenger* had exploded and that Captain Bartholomew had called, requesting my services. He wanted me to fly to DC, get briefed by NASA, and then fly with him down to Cape Canaveral. That day, I flew into DC, greeted Captain Bartholomew, and went into a series of meetings with senators, congressmen, NASA senior leadership, Air Force generals, and Navy admirals.

Having the chance to observe "Black Bart" in action was a crash course in leadership during a crisis. I had never seen someone who was so calm and masterful during a crisis, all the while not losing sight of the most important details and ensuring that everyone knew what to do, how to do it, and when to do it. By the time the meetings were over, he was able to get the Air Force to give operational control to the Navy and NASA to provide whatever space he needed and any number of people he needed. To my surprise, "Black Bart" indicated he would need only about seven or eight people. He brought them together quickly and set up headquarters in less than a day. Over the ensuing crisis and recovery of the crash, he reported by pay phone directly to the White House each day and briefed the entire press corps every evening, taking the time to patiently, thoroughly, and respectfully answer any questions. To me, this drove home an important point about leadership. Regardless of the situation, something can be done about it, and as dire as the situation is, there is only one way to go, and that is "up." During this entire time, your demeanor, reaction, and "quickness on your feet" is just as important as the actions taken, since your example serves as a beacon of hope and inspiration to those around you.

It is in our nature to resist change, and, for some of us, it is very scary. However, change is the essence of life, and you need to master yourself so that you can handle change when it occurs and adapt as necessary. One of my biggest life changes happened after 26 years of getting up and putting on a uniform. It was not of my choosing; it was thrust on me, and it began the transition for me from a military to a civilian career. Six months into my tour at Long Beach Naval Shipyard, BRAC was implemented. For those of you not familiar with the lexicon, BRAC stands for Base Realignment and Closure, the congressionally authorized process within the Department of Defense to reorganize its base structure to be more efficient and effective. In other words, they were shutting down a lot of military bases, and Long Beach was one of them. A few weeks later, the Secretary of Labor visited us and told everyone our shipyard would be shut down in two years; we had to fire 5,500 people. We were given a check to cover closing costs, and that was that.

Hearkening back to my time with "Black Bart," I was determined to make this an "up" experience for our employees. Each one of them had families to support, children to send to school, and their own set of hopes and dreams. I was not content with just simply letting them go, and neither were the rest of the folks with me. We took action and put together a team to research and develop programs and processes for our employees for seeking and finding employment. We established career counseling, helped them with resumes, even financial planning, and put together job fairs—fourteen in all. While it was an emotional time, filled with angst for many, we did not leave anyone behind or let someone fall into despair. Eventually, every single employee found employment, and, to this day, I look back and see this as one of my proudest accomplishments. It would have been easy to simply go through the motions and not make the extra effort and take the time to help everyone, but a true leader has the team's best interests in mind at all times and walks the talk.

As it turned out, the job fairs had an unintended benefit for me as well. At one of our first job fairs, as I was standing there in my uniform, a gentleman came up to me, handed me his card, and said, "I'll give you 150 to be our PM." I thanked him, although for what I didn't know, and immediately went over to the leader of our placement team and asked what "150 to be our PM" meant. She laughed and informed me that 150 was $150,000 and a PM was a Project Manager. I was stunned, as it was more than double my current salary, and while it was flattering to know that someone was interested in me, I never accepted the position because I was still on active duty, and I was not interested in being a PM. As the closing of the shipyard wound down, I received my orders, and, after twenty-six years, decided to leave the military and enter the civilian world. The reasons for my decision were twofold. My next duty assignment would be in Washington, DC. I had never seen myself as a Beltway guy, plus I didn't want to relocate again, as I really liked where I was living. Secondly, it was time to move on and do something different. I had an urge to try my hand at something else and see if I could replicate my success in the civilian world.

However, once the decision to leave Naval service was made, the next one wasn't that easy. I literally had no idea what I wanted to do since I never had to choose; when you're in the Navy, you receive your orders and accept whatever job or leadership position you are assigned. After numerous discussions with many of my friends and mentors, I realized I thrived when I had command or ownership. I reached the conclusion that I ultimately wanted to be a President or CEO in my next career, although of what and where I had no idea. I did realize that any aspirations to attain this type of position would be buttressed by getting a Master of Business Administration (MBA) degree, something several of my mentors strongly recommended. With this goal in mind, I then had two issues to act on. One was to secure a job that would give me the responsibility and authority to test my mettle in the civilian world and potentially be a springboard for my ultimate goal. The other was to provide income so I could pay for an MBA, and in concert with that, to apply and get accepted to a program for an MBA.

Taking things in order, I commenced my job search. The Naval Academy Alumni Association had established a resource to help graduates with their post-military job. This resource was called the SABRD, or Service Academy Business Resource Directory. It lists every military-academy graduate, tells you if these people are interested in helping someone with a transition, and where they are currently working. There were more than 30 pages of names, hundreds in all, and I called each and every one of them. One of the first batch of calls included Jim Kelly, a USNA graduate. I wasn't very good at the whole prospecting thing over the phone and recalled someone advising me not to ask for a job, but, instead, to play it low key and get them talking about themselves. After stumbling through the initial part of the phone conversation, I decided to get him talking about himself and asked him if he liked what he was doing. Wrong question! At first, he said, "Why in the hell would you care? followed by "Do I sound like the type of person who would be doing something I didn't like?" He then told me my telephone skills were terrible (or words to that effect) and asked if I was a PE (Professional Engineer). I told him I was and had worked in engineering positions for more than 20 years. He barked "Send me your resume" and ended the conversation.

As it turned out, I was later offered a job by Jim Kelly. The job was with the Metropolitan Water District, and I was to be one of five Directors, all reporting to the Chief Operating Officer, who was Jim. The MWD has thousands of employees, nearly 250 managers, a vast territory, and dozens of facilities, so each director had a large area of responsibility, with hundreds of people. It was here that I had my first mentor outside of the Navy, and it was none other than Jim Kelly himself. He took me under his wing, showed me the ins and outs of the business, critiqued me when I was doing something wrong, and led me in the right direction. As the newest Director of the five, I was still very much learning my way around and was fortunate to have Jill Wicke as a mentor. She, too, took me under her wing, so to speak, and was a valuable ongoing source of inspiration and guidance. This was especially admirable to me, since she had worked at MWD for more than 30 years to get her position, and there wasn't one bit of professional envy or resentment.

Between Jim and Jill, their advice and guidance enabled me to come up to speed quickly. At the same time, I discovered that the Peter Drucker School of Business at Claremont University was only a ten-minute drive from my office at the MWD. I applied, was accepted, went to night school, and finished my MBA in two years. It was here that I had the privilege of meeting Jean Lipman-Blumen, who taught my first class. Jean was one of the first women to graduate from Harvard Business School, was Ronald Reagan's representative to the World Peace Conference, and had published numerous books on my favorite topic—leadership. In particular, her book *The Connective Edge* reinforced in me the need to shift your leadership style from situation to situation and from person to person; the leader who was able to do this adroitly had a decided advantage. Jean was my third mentor outside the Navy. We spent countless hours discussing skills that were transferrable from the military to civilian life—of which all are, I might add—and importantly, invested time with me to help me develop those areas where she perceived I had a shortfall.

My success at the MWD with the lessons learned and applied, in conjunction with the MBA experience and my extensive military experience provided the impetus for me to receive offers for more senior positions with different companies. After a while, having done all that I needed to do at MWD, I was ready for new challenges in more senior leadership positions. I will spare you the details, but I was pleased that I was able to mirror my success in the military as I ultimately achieved my goal of becoming a President and CEO. Once again, I had reverted to form, as I did when I chose option three as my career path. I had a goal, I was committed, I acted on it, and I had the discipline and resiliency to persevere. It was also obvious to me that, in addition to these traits and characteristics necessary for success, there are two other points which deserve further emphasis and which I would urge someone to follow. The first is that I would encourage anyone who aspires to a position of responsibility to be proactive when it comes to finding mentors, as their counsel will be proven to be valuable, time and time again. The second is recognition and action. In other words, you need to understand that there are things you plan, and there are things that happen. The recognition of those things that happen is important, because, in many instances, those opportunities do not come gift wrapped, but they present themselves, nonetheless. At that juncture, the courage and ability to act on those opportunities, versus staying in your comfort zone, makes all the difference in the world.

Back on the subject of mentors, I save the best for last and would be remiss if I didn't recognize and acknowledge the most important mentor I have ever had—Amy Breen—who happens to also be my wife. Amy Breen is one of the most dynamic leaders I have ever met. She was one of the first people to come onboard a small company of a couple of dozen people; she launched what would become the branded division of Teva Pharmaceuticals. Her leadership resulted in her team achieving the highest ranking in the world on more than one occasion, and she has received too many personal awards and accolades for sales and leadership to name. On more than one occasion, when I was faced with a difficult situation or had a decision to make, her guidance and counsel helped me find the way. I am blessed and grateful for her support and love. Having Amy in my life also reinforced to me the importance of having a life partner who is there to help you. I can't imagine how I would have been able to get anything accomplished without her by my side.

I trust that sharing my story will help provide you with further insight and inspiration in whatever stage you are in during your leadership career. We all have it in us to be leaders, however, it doesn't come naturally. You have to work at it, listen and learn in the best environment with the best leaders and mentors possible, and discover what works for you, all the while being true to yourself and not trying to be something you are not. It is eminently doable, but it starts with you, and if you adhere to the advice I have laid out, it is certainly a good start. In addition to this, in closing, I leave you with one further recommendation, which is a piece of advice my parents continually reinforced in me and which has served me well throughout my life and my career: "Do the right thing, for the right reason, at the right time." I wish you Godspeed. With best wishes, Alan.

CHAPTER SIXTEEN

GENERATIONS

★ ★ ★ ★ ★

"I see no hope for the future of our people if they are dependent on frivolous youth of today, for certainly all youth are reckless beyond words. When I was young, we were taught to be discreet and respectful of elders, but the present youth are exceedingly disrespectful and impatient of restraint."—Hesiod, 8th century BC.

★ ★ ★ ★ ★

THE MORE THINGS CHANGE, the more they remain the same. The above is a quote from approximately 10,000 years ago, expressing frustration and dismay with the youth of that day. Fast forward, and you see the same sentiments expressed about the youth of today—their attitude, characteristics, work ethic, and their perceived ability, or lack thereof, to contribute to society and be useful and productive citizens. The "youth today" as it relates to this chapter, will focus on the Millennials and Generation Z. This segment, which is anyone born from 1982 onward, comprises more than half of our population, and correspondingly, a higher and higher share of our workforce.

The overarching challenge for a leader today is a generational issue. An effective leader needs to understand what motivates this segment and how to relate to them. This is even more important due to the transformation of business and the global economy. In former times, it was much more common for someone to seek a job at a company with the goal of securing a career, with implied lifelong benefits and security. Those days are gone, since, by the time the average person hits their early to mid-thirties, they will have worked for at least three to five companies. Moreover, there is a stronger desire to become self-reliant from an employment standpoint. With technology and connectivity, someone is just as apt to try to start up their own company or work freelance as they are to work for a company. As a result, these individuals will succeed, fail, survive, or thrive based on the sum of their experience and the training they have received. With this segment, there are also deeper issues that differentiate them from earlier generations that need to be considered and given the proper context. This relates to two areas. First is how they were raised, and second, the unparalleled role technology has played in their life versus former generations.

The first issue is the way many were raised. Many parents had fewer material advantages as children and struggled to get to the point where they could provide for their children, but they provided for them in such a manner that it thwarted their development. They went all out for their children, placing them in programs and activities which touted their achievement at an early stage. Being placed in TAG (Talent and Gifted) programs, often at their parents' behest, being told they were special, and receiving medals and trophies for simply showing up and participating reinforced the fact that everyone was special, everyone was a winner. Moreover, in most instances, there was money for a service provided, and the schools and universities, having a vested interest in them getting the highest scores and succeeding in class, did everything they could to accommodate them, ensuring they would pass. The higher the grades, the higher the graduation rate, the happier the students and, just as importantly, the parents. Today, students are told "don't worry," "everything will be all right," "it's not your fault," "it's not fair"—they are told what to think, not how to think. It seems like a real win-win, but it isn't, which is setting them up for a difficult path after graduation.

After graduation, the role is reversed. They are employed and paid for their services. They are expected to perform and, in many cases, are left to their own devices. They are held accountable, critiqued, and criticized. They no longer feel special. One can only imagine how they must feel, since they are in this environment devoid of any coping mechanism. Experiencing adversity and failure is a learning experience and part of someone's development. If you have never experienced adversity and failure, and if you've never developed resiliency, it is important to understand the drivers, develop coping mechanisms, and become mentally tough. It doesn't happen overnight, but with awareness and action, it is eminently doable, as it is a matter of learning and training.

Secondly is social media and technology. This is a very contrived and filtered existence, and, in most cases, it's not real. You can manufacture a profile and experience. You friend someone, they friend you, it adds up. You post something, you get likes and comments—almost instantly—and you get that dopamine hit. You are popular. You feel great. You are addicted and continue the cycle. You want to ask someone out—you text them. You want to break up with someone—you text them, message them online, ghost them, or block them. Communication is in bits and bytes, face-to-face discussion becomes rarer, and you don't take the time to develop those relationships and have those conversations, especially the tough ones, that solicit a better understanding and form the bonds of a relationship. In this age, when so many are connected and can differentiate themselves through what they wear, how they label themselves, and how they describe themselves, people are more isolated and lost than ever. You don't know what's going on in someone else's mind. It creates fear and confusion, so it's simply easier to cut someone off as opposed to having that tough conversation. This comes home to roost later, when circumstances are different, and you are in a different environment.

For a leader to be effective, it is important for a leader to be adaptive, embrace ideas from the entire spectrum, and understand what inspires and motivates them. By developing a better understanding, the leader can better relate to and lead them in the most effective manner possible. To develop a better understanding of this segment, a leadership course was designed at the University of San Diego to provide insight into these issues. The project was implemented with two classes. There was a combined total of 25 students. The students were given a list of questions to get their views on a range of issues pertaining to leadership, which they all submitted toward the end of the semester. The class was held via Zoom, accompanied by robust question-and-answer sessions.

The questionnaire covered a range of topics, such as the definition of leadership, are leaders born or made, what the characteristics of an effective leader are, what experiences helped shaped their personality, the biggest challenge a leader faces, what the most effective leadership style is, their opinion on leadership training, what their goals are, and what motivates them. At the end of the semester, I presented my analysis and recommendations to the class, which are listed verbatim below.

The responses from the students were insightful, with many common denominators. For this discussion, the term "many" means "more than 50%," and the term "majority" means "more than 75%."

The majority of the students made a strong connection between success and leadership. They felt that, for someone to lead, he or she must be proficient and accomplished, which imbues confidence and respect, with self-confidence being an important aspect. The majority believed leaders are developed and shaped by their experience and learning, and that, with some people, it comes easier due to their personality. Inspiration, motivation, and setting the example were listed by the majority of the students as desirable qualities in a leader. Parents, teachers, and sports were all listed as being primary influencers. It was refreshing to see their responses devoid of the leadership lexicon of buzzwords such as *transformative, servant,* etc. Not one person even mentioned a specific leadership style, and the majority of students opined that, due to the differences in people and circumstances, there is no one-size-fits-all style. The majority were keen on leadership training and were pointed in their desire to learn from someone who has experience. The majority of the students professed a desire to become proficient in their field and wanted to make a difference. Very few expressed regrets and were thankful for past experiences and decisions, as it helped shaped their views. In terms of challenges or obstacles, a common denominator for many were decisions made or not made due to fear.

Based on the questionnaires, the class sessions, and the question-and-answer sessions, I addressed each class with a summary and wrap-up. My goal was to give them something specific and actionable. I covered a range of issues, and, for the purpose of retaining the integrity of those remarks, I list them verbatim below.

In terms of what characteristics and values you believe constitute effective leadership and would find motivating, I list the following topics:

1. **Communication.** Communication was right up there on every response. You want to be heard, and you value a leader who will listen so that you have a chance to express your views and offer your input.
2. **Inspiration.** Someone who sets a good example, is a role model, and motivates you.
3. **Trust.** You want someone who has integrity, who has your back, and who won't throw you under the bus.
4. **Empathy.** You want to be understood, your circumstances noted, emotions understood, and want a leader with compassion.
5. **Decision-making.** The autocratic style won't work well with you. You want to know *why* something is being done, the logic behind it, your role in it, and you want to be a part of the decision-making process.

6. **Adaptability.** You were quite attuned to the fact that each person is different, each situation is different, and there is no cookie-cutter approach when it comes to leadership and how a person is to be handled or a situation addressed.

7. **Humility.** In line with your desire to avoid the "Dark Triad" personality, you value a leader who is humble and self-effacing, with his or her interests subservient to the welfare of the entire group and mission.

8. **Attitude.** You will not do well with a doom-and-gloom mentality. You want someone who is positive and exudes confidence, even in the face of adversity or failure. You find this trait very inspiring. The term "grace under pressure" fits well here.

9. **Empowerment.** You want to be given the goal or parameters, the necessary means, and the latitude to do your job, bereft of micromanagement or simply being told "do this or do that."

10. **Respect.** You want to be recognized for your abilities and trusted to complete the task or attain the objective; you want your achievements acknowledged.

For you to be successful and develop your leadership skills, I make these recommendations:

1. **Alignment.** If you believe, it will help you achieve. Many of you desire to be a part of something, to make a difference, and have an impact. With you, it is not so much about the money as it is about the mission. Consequently, the greater you align your interests,

beliefs, and skill set, the better the fit and the greater the prospects for success. This staunch belief and commitment will help you weather adversity and deal with failures.

2. **Environment.** It is important to insert yourself into an environment where the mission, values, and standard practices are consistent with your beliefs and values. It should also be an environment where you are challenged and can become a better person. This continual reinforcement will ingrain habits and instill discipline, which are the underpinnings for success. The same holds true for those you associate with, so choose wisely, and avoid groupthink.

3. **Perseverance.** Be patient. Understand that something worthwhile takes time. Put your instant-gratification impulses on hold, and be willing to not only make the effort but put in the time for you and things to develop. Honor the struggle, and struggle well. It will help you develop the mental toughness and resilience required for your journey.

4. **Goal setting.** One of the traits of successful people is that they set goals for both their professional and personal life. These goals give you a sense of direction and motivate you. Continually review, adapt, and relentlessly pursue your goals. Strive for progress, not perfection.

5. **Challenge yourself.** There is a great deal of truth to the adage "No discomfort = No growth." For you to grow, you need to continually challenge yourself and face your fears. By doing this, you eliminate the

barriers, learn from your experience, build on it, gain
confidence, and prepare yourself to do it again.

6. **Adversity and failure.** All of you will face varying
degrees of adversity in your lives. You can't run from
it, hide from it, or avoid it. You must accept it as a
learning experience, act, and move on. How you deal
with adversity could be viewed as the single biggest
challenge in your life. The same holds true for failure.
This is part of life and part of the spectrum of success.
With each failure, there is a lesson learned, and it is
proof you are trying.

7. **Decision-making.** Make quality decisions. Make
decisions for the right reasons, based on what you
want to happen as opposed to what you want to avoid.
Consider the desired outcome and what value it brings,
and have a contingency plan in place, as things don't
always work out the way we envision. Ensure that you
get as much information as possible, be objective, avoid
confirmation bias, and understand that, even if the
decision is imperfect, you can make a course correction
and continue to move forward.

8. **Authenticity.** Do not try to be something you are not.
Take time to pursue meaningful activities with tangible
results that add value. Set a positive example, be a team
player, be humble, and be a person of integrity always.
Develop meaningful relationships, manage your time
on social media, and set boundaries. Learn to say "No"
instead of "Maybe."

9. **Mentors.** No one has all the answers, and that includes
you. Have the presence of mind and the strength to

ask for help and solicit opinions from others. Strive to have one or more mentors who you can talk with, commiserate with, and solicit input from. Learn to be comfortable with constructive criticism, and look at it as an opportunity to grow as opposed to bristling at the comments.

10. **Tolerance and respect.** Be tolerant and respectful at all times. Avoid rushes to judgment. Seek the truth, and speak the truth. Find common ground when you can and appreciate that it is those different points of view that enable us to understand various perspectives and other opinions. A respectful discourse, as opposed to assailing the other person's point of view simply because it does not fit your narrative, only widens the divide. Politics, religion, and other such matters are private and have no place in the work environment; they should not form the basis for determining who is a friend and who is not.

In closing, there is one thing I *don't* want you to do, and I am taking a quote from the *The Power of 3: Lessons in Leadership,* written by one of my classmates, Steven Mays. In his book, Steven expresses the need to "Drive Despair Out," which is precisely what you should do. I do not want you to despair. Quite the opposite. You are the brightest, most intelligent group this country has produced. You have the means, but you need to find the way. Darwin stated, "It is not the strong who survive, but those who adapt." That will certainly be the case here and will be the key to your success and becoming a leader. Recognize what is important, take the necessary action, and adapt. Each of you have it within you to get there. So go for it—and may you have fair winds and following seas on your journey.

CONCLUSION

*"Speakers who talk about what life has taught them
never fail to keep the attention of their listeners."*
—Dale Carnegie

★ ★ ★ ★ ★

CONCLUSIONS SHOULD BE BRIEF AND TO THE POINT, which is what I will do.

I read the above quote a few years ago. This got the wheels turning and was the genesis for this book. Whatever walk of life we are in, we can learn from others. And what better way is there to learn leadership than from individuals who have that experience, have been successful, and are willing to share it with you?

I would like to thank you for taking the time to read the stories of the remarkable men and women in this book. I trust I was able to accomplish the three things I mentioned in the introduction:

1. Help the reader become a great leader by learning new perspectives on leadership
2. Provide guidance on principles and practices that have been proven to work in a number of environments
3. Motivate and inspire the reader

I would like to leave you with a few words of advice. There is a strong connection between success and leadership, as mentioned earlier. Toward that end, I will use my AEP acronym, which represents three fundamental issues that are central to your success. Strive to attain the best degree of **A**lignment possible, insert yourself in the best **E**nvironment possible, and **P**ersevere, honoring the struggle. With respect to your leadership, remember that all leadership is situational, and your manner of behaving and leading is based on numerous factors, all of which are constantly changing. I have never been a big fan of leadership styles, but if you need one for yourself, you should be an *Adaptive Leader*. And never forget that, while there are timeless principles and techniques that stand the test of time and will always remain relevant as best practices, leadership is unique to everyone, and you must strive to find what pattern works best for you.

Once again, thank you for taking the time to read *The Experience of Leadership*. I wish you all the best in your leadership journey. If this book can help contribute to your leadership journey, then mine has been worth it.

Respectfully,
Fred Stuvek, Jr.

About the Author

Fred Stuvek, Jr. has achieved extraordinary success in diverse realms. Born in West Virginia and raised in Pennsylvania, he has been inducted into the Pennsylvania Sports Hall of Fame for achievements in football, basketball, baseball, and track. He graduated from the United States Naval Academy, after lettering three years as quarterback for the Midshipmen. After service as a Naval Officer, he transitioned to the business world where he has held senior leadership positions in private and public companies, both domestically and internationally. Key successes include an international medical imaging start-up that led to a successful IPO, and forming a private medical services company, which he subsequently sold. His first book, It Starts With You: Turn Your Goals Into Success, is one of the top ranked books for self-development, garnering praise for its no nonsense approach to going after what you want out of life. From the playing field, to the war room, to the board room his leadership and accomplishments have given him a distinct perspective and a results-oriented mindset. To learn more about Fred and his work, please visit www.fredstuvek.com.

Made in the USA
Monee, IL
06 November 2023